Quiet Strength: Uncovering Resilience Through Life's Storms

Megan Sharisse

Quiet Strength: Uncovering Resilience Through Life's Storms
Copyright © 2025 Megan Sharisse

Library of Congress Control Number: 2025909955

Paperback ISBN: (print only) 979-8-9989804-0-4

Hardback ISBN: (print only) 979-8-9909804-1-1

Cover Art by: JoBella Dezignz

Edited by: Naomi Books, LLC

Printed in the United States of America

Dedication

Grandma, although you are no longer with us, this book is lovingly dedicated to you. Throughout the years we shared, you taught me strength, kindness, and resilience. Your quiet strength inspired me in more ways than you could ever imagine. The love and wisdom you poured into my life remain a guiding force, even in your absence. I carry your lessons in my heart and strive every day to make you proud.

Mama, thank you for your unwavering support, endless love, and the countless sacrifices you've made. This book is a testament to your belief in me and my dreams. Thank you for always being my greatest inspiration.

To all those who are navigating their own storms and seeking a glimmer of hope in the darkest clouds—this book is for you. May you find solace in knowing that every obstacle you face holds within it the seeds of resilience and growth. As you journey through these pages, I hope you discover that even the fiercest storms have a silver lining, and with each storm weathered, you grow stronger and more radiant. Your strength and courage are your guiding lights, and may this book inspire you to trust that brighter days are always on the horizon.

Table of Contents

Introduction... 1

Chapter 1 Against All Odds: My Journey from Wreckage to Resilience.. 4

Chapter 2 The Road to the Classroom: A Dream Realized Through Faith and Resilience... 21

Chapter 3 When Teaching Becomes Personal: The Student Who Taught Me Resilience 33

Chapter 4 Echoes of Fragility: Confronting Life's Unpredictability 47

Chapter 5 From Closure to Connection: Teaching Beyond Classroom Walls 71

Chapter 6 Holding On to Hope: Trusting God's Report.. 87

Chapter 7 Trials Amid Turmoil: Battling Health and the Workplace.. 103

Chapter 8 A Leap of Faith: Embracing Change and New Opportunities.. 124

Chapter 9 Facing the Storm: Resilience and Resolve in the Classroom... 139

Chapter 10 A New Beginning: Trusting the Journey Ahead 165

Acknowledgments... 182

About the Author 184

Introduction

Life is full of uncertainties—events that nobody can predict or plan for. We have all experienced those moments where unplanned events left us feeling overwhelmed, uncertain, or completely depleted. How do we find the strength to overcome these challenges? Rest assured, God does not play favorites. He offers the same strength and resilience to all His children, including you.

My journey began with a life-altering event: a severe head trauma that I miraculously survived. The road to recovery was long and arduous, marked by countless challenges that tested my strength and spirit. But survive I did, discovering an inner resilience and a deep faith in God that would become my guiding light.

Driven by a passion for making a difference, I pursued a career in teaching. The classroom became my sanctuary, a place where I could channel my energy and make a lasting impact on young lives. Yet, life had more trials in store for me. As I navigated my teaching journey, I faced a series of storms that would have brought many to their knees. While each of these crises was a reminder of my vulnerability, they were also a testament to the incredible strength that faith and resilience can provide.

Through every storm I faced, I continued to show up. I showed up for my students, my family, and myself, pouring my heart into everything and everyone despite the uncertainties and fears that loomed over me. Teaching became more than just a profession; it was my lifeline, a testament to my strength, perseverance, and unwavering faith in God.

Even in silence, I was being strengthened.

Now, as I embrace a new chapter in my life, I am compelled to share my story. This memoir is a chronicle of my journey—a story of overcoming immense physical and emotional obstacles while maintaining my commitment to education and my students. It's about finding purpose in the face of adversity and the unshakable belief that with God, all things are possible.

As I reflect on my path, I see not just the challenges I've faced, but the resilience, hope, and faith that have carried me through. This is my story, a testament to the power of perseverance, the impact of one teacher's unwavering spirit, and the boundless possibilities that faith in God can unlock.

My hope is that through my experiences, you, too, will find the strength to overcome your own trials and the faith to believe that with God, all things are possible.

As you read, I invite you to consider how God might be equipping you—even now—to stand strong through your own storms.

Chapter 1

Against All Odds: My Journey from Wreckage to Resilience

"What is a miracle?"

This question, posed during a children's church service nearly two decades ago, still lingers in my memory. I shyly raised my hand and whispered, "A special happening."

I didn't fully grasp the depth of those words then, but little did I know—one day, I would come to understand their true meaning. I would experience a miracle firsthand, surviving a near-fatal car accident that left me with a resilience and determination I never knew I possessed.

The Day Everything Changed

May 9, 2004 (Mother's Day), began like any other Sunday. I woke up with a sense of excitement and responsibility, eager to fulfill my role in leading the Mother's Day Responsive Reading at church. I carefully chose a teal two-piece skirt set, its fabric shimmering softly in the morning light, and tied my hair back with a matching ribbon, completing the look that made me feel confident and prepared.

As my mom, grandma, older brother, and I headed to church, the familiar scent of Elizabeth Taylor's White Diamond filled the car, mingling with the gentle hum of gospel music on the radio. The drive was peaceful, the spring air crisp and full of promise. When we arrived, the sight of the brick church with its towering steeple and the warm greetings of the congregation made me feel right at home. Inside, the sweet smiles of church members and the choir's harmonious voices lifted in praise filled the sanctuary, creating an atmosphere of joy and reverence.

The service went off without a hitch, and everything felt perfectly in place. As was our tradition, a fellow church member had prepared a special Mother's Day meal for us to pick up after the service. Although we'd already had plans for a family Mother's Day dinner, my mom mentioned we'd stop by on our way home, a familiar routine on this special day. We got into the car, anticipation in the air, and then my memory went blank. The next thing I recalled was waking up in a hospital bed nearly two weeks later. My life forever changed.

I vividly remember the morning the nurses came in to remove the staples from my head, although I had awakened from a week-and-a-half-long coma just a few days prior. A combination of stitches and staples held me together, but only the staples needed to be taken out as the stitches were designed to dissolve on their own. The removal process, although simple, was accompanied by a stinging pain that reminded me of the severity of my ordeal.

I had been told that I was involved in a car accident on May 9th. We were rear-ended by a driver who had experienced a medical issue while driving. The collision left me with such severe head trauma that I had to be airlifted to a hospital in Columbia, South Carolina, which was better equipped to handle my injuries. Thankfully, the impact left me unconscious because there was no other way I would have gotten into that helicopter. In our small town, the emergency team initially struggled to find a suitable landing spot for the helicopter, but they quickly turned to the local high school football field, providing a timely solution.

Emergency surgery was necessary to address a skull fracture, which caused significant bleeding and pressure on my brain. My mom recounted how, after the collision, she could see that my brother was alright, and she could hear my grandma, but I was unresponsive. When she glanced back toward me, I briefly lifted my head, smiled faintly, and then my head went further back as blood poured from my nose, eyes, and head.

To repair the skull fracture, surgeons had to shave the right side of my head, leaving a scar that ran from my forehead around to my right ear. My Aunt Leah and Uncle Larry, at whose house we were planning to have dinner on that day, had to leave their home and drive to the hospital to give consent for the life-saving procedures since my mother and grandmother were transported by ambulance to a different facility.

Years later, my Aunt Francena shared a conversation with me about the accident. She told me that when they initially contacted the hospital that Sunday, they were told to arrive urgently due to my critical condition. It was so dire that a local newspaper erroneously reported that I had died from the accident. We were also told, given the force of the impact and where the car was struck, that it was nothing short of a miracle that the car didn't explode.

Upon my arrival at the hospital, doctors were uncertain about my survival. After the surgeries, when I emerged from the coma, they worried about my ability to function normally. They even speculated that I might not finish school or, if I did, I might not be able to thrive in a regular classroom setting.

Though the staples were eventually removed, and I showed signs of progress, there were still concerns about my vision. The blunt force trauma and the impact of the surgery had caused my right eye to turn backward, rendering me temporarily blind in that eye. I was advised to wear a patch to shield it from direct light and prevent further damage. My memory was also affected; I couldn't recall much from before the day the staples were removed.

At the moment the staples were removed, the meaning of "a special happening" became all too real to me. I had survived something that *should* have taken my life, and I emerged with a renewed understanding of what it means to face life's greatest obstacles. *This* was my miracle, a reminder that even in our darkest moments, there is hope, and through faith and resilience, we can overcome the unimaginable.

Day by day, appointment after appointment, I made progress and was finally discharged from the hospital. The real test began as I had to function outside the controlled environment of the hospital. The week of my discharge coincided with my promotional exercises, marking my transition from middle school to high school. I had missed all the practices and events leading up to the ceremony, but thankfully, our caps and gowns had been ordered months earlier. This was officially my first time being out in public following my accident.

My mom drove me to the high school where the ceremony would take place. As I walked in, my friends and classmates greeted me with excitement, countless hugs, tears of joy, and heartfelt "I missed you" messages. When it was time to march in, I took my place in line behind one of my best friends and followed him as he led the way. The applause that erupted when I entered the gymnasium was overwhelming—a testament to the journey I had endured and the support that surrounded me.

Reflecting on this experience, I am reminded of **Isaiah 40:31 (NIV): "... but those who hope in the LORD will renew their strength. They will soar on wings like eagles; they will run and not grow weary, they will walk and not be faint."** Despite the grim predictions and the immense obstacles, I persevered with faith and determination, demonstrating that through God's grace, resilience, and the support of loved ones, we can overcome any obstacle and move forward with hope.

Throughout that summer, my friends and classmates were attending summer camps and engaging in exciting activities. Although I desperately wanted to, I was unable to join them. My days were filled with trips back and forth to Columbia for follow-up appointments and head CT scans. My mom, tirelessly and hopefully, drove me to these appointments, where I constantly felt like a pincushion, being poked and prodded by doctors, ensuring everything was progressing well.

As August approached, the time came for me to begin my freshman year of high school. I recall the meeting that summer when my mom had to discuss the possibility of an Individualized Education Program (IEP) or a 504 Plan for me. Both plans are designed to address the needs of individuals with physical, medical, or cognitive conditions that directly impact their education. After much discussion, it was agreed that I would have a 504 Plan.

Thanks to my determination to overcome and a strong faith in God's healing power, I did not need special education services. However, it was recommended that I receive certain accommodations in the educational setting, such as extended time on classwork, repeated directions, and seating close to the point of instruction. These adjustments were vital in ensuring I could navigate my school environment successfully. I was determined *not* to need those accommodations because I did not want to be treated differently by my teachers. I was resolute in proving I could keep up with my peers, so I continued to take honors classes alongside my friends. It was important to me to tackle the same rigorous coursework and participate fully in discussions, group projects, and challenging assignments. The only exceptions were certain activities in Physical Education (PE) class. Given the head trauma I had experienced, I avoided activities that could potentially cause further injury or undo the progress I had made.

Each day, I was reminded of **Romans 12:2 (NIV): "Do not conform to the pattern of this world, but be transformed by the renewing of your mind…"** I embraced this mindset, knowing that my strength and perseverance were setting me apart. I worked tirelessly, not only to keep up with my friends but also to excel and demonstrate that my abilities were not defined by my injury. This drive and determination made me stronger, both academically and personally, as I navigated my high school years with resilience and faith.

I can vividly remember feeling very self-conscious about my new haircut and the prominent scar that ran across my head. To help with my anxiety, I was allowed to wear a hat during classes. One day, however, a teacher, unaware of my situation, told me to remove the hat because hats were against school policy. I tried to explain, but she insisted I take it off. This was the first time most people saw the scar on my head because I had always worn hats since the day I left the hospital. Reluctantly, I took the hat off, feeling extremely exposed and insecure.

After class, I ran into one of the school counselors. She noticed immediately that my hat was missing and asked why. I explained what had happened in class. She reassured me, "Put your hat back on. I'll make sure this doesn't happen again." True to her word, I never had to remove my hat again during school.

Despite the relief, I still felt the weight of my insecurities. One of my "big sisters" at school noticed my discomfort and offered to help. She braided my hair in a way that helped mask the scar, giving me a bit more confidence. This small act of kindness made a significant difference in my self-esteem and reminded me of **Psalm 147:3 (NIV): "He heals the brokenhearted and binds up their wounds."**

With each braid, I felt a little more healed, both physically and emotionally, and learned to embrace my journey and scars as part of my unique story.

I finished the year normally, maintaining an A/B average in my classes. The following three years went by much the same, filled with the typical ups and downs of high school life. After my freshman year, I no longer needed the 504 Plan support or permission to wear a hat. In a bold move of confidence, I decided to cut my hair, and it eventually grew back stronger and healthier.

I continued to excel academically and socially. By the time I reached my junior year, I had already completed all the required courses for graduation. Along with a few classmates, I was offered the opportunity to graduate a year early. However, we declined, choosing instead to finish our high school journey with the friends who had supported us along the way.

On June 5, 2008, I graduated with the fourth-highest honor in my class. Standing on that stage, diploma in hand, I felt a profound sense of accomplishment. I had overcome so much and was now ready to face the next phase, which was college.

Emerging from this ordeal with my life intact was nothing short of miraculous. The doctors' grim predictions became the fuel for my resilience. Day by day, I defied their expectations, determined to prove I could recover and thrive. This experience taught me that, like a miracle, resilience is a special happening, an inner strength that enables us to bend without breaking. It reminds us that no matter how dire the circumstances, the human spirit is capable of extraordinary things.

As I reflect on this journey, I am reminded of **Jeremiah 29:11 (NIV): "For I know the plans I have for you,' declares the LORD, 'plans to prosper you and not to harm you, plans to give you hope and a future."** Every step of the way, God had a plan for me, guiding and supporting me through the toughest times. My story is a testament to His grace and the power of resilience.

The journey from that devastating car accident to my high school graduation was a path paved with trials, faith, and perseverance. I am a walking miracle, a living testament to the power of resilience and the grace of God. As I move forward into the next chapter of my life, I carry with me the unshakable belief that God's work in me is not finished yet. My story, like so many others, is a beacon of hope and a reminder that, with faith and determination, we can overcome any obstacle.

Reflection Questions

1. What does the word "miracle" mean to you?

_____

_____

_____

_____

_____

_____

_____

_____

Have you ever experienced or witnessed something you would consider a *miracle*?

_____

_____

_____

_____

_____

_____

_____

_____

2. How do you find strength in the face of overwhelming challenges?

_____

_____

_____

_____

_____

_____

_____

_____

What role does faith or belief play in that process?

_____

_____

_____

_____

_____

_____

_____

_____

_____

3. In moments of adversity, how do you remind yourself of your inner resilience?

_____

_____

_____

_____

_____

_____

_____

_____

What personal experiences reinforce your ability to overcome?

_____

_____

_____

_____

_____

_____

_____

_____

_____

4. What scars—physical or emotional—have you carried with you?

_____

_____

_____

_____

_____

_____

_____

_____

_____

How have those scars shaped your journey toward healing and self-acceptance?

_____

_____

_____

_____

_____

_____

_____

_____

_____

5. Reflect on a time when you felt guided or supported by a higher power, the universe, or your own inner strength.

   How did that guidance impact your path forward?

   _____

   _____

   _____

   _____

   _____

   _____

   _____

   _____

   _____

   _____

   _____

   _____

   _____

   _____

   _____

   _____

   _____

Chapter 2

The Road to the Classroom: A Dream Realized Through Faith and Resilience

F rom a young age, I knew I was destined to be a teacher. My earliest memories are filled with "playing school" with my younger cousins, Chelsea and Amanda, assigning them roles as students while I eagerly took on the part of the teacher. Armed with a chalkboard and makeshift worksheets, I would mimic the lessons I had learned in school, delighting in the opportunity to share knowledge and guide their pretend "learning journeys." Yet, I wasn't just playing a game; I was practicing for a future I fervently believed in. As I grew older, this passion only intensified. Teaching wasn't just a career choice; it was a calling that resonated with every fiber of my being.

* * *

I can vividly recall the day I received a notification from the Education Testing Service (ETS) informing me that my recent Principles of Learning and Teaching (PLT) scores had become available. Passing this test was the final hurdle standing between me and the commencement of my student teaching journey in the upcoming fall semester. To provide some context, the Department of Teacher Education at my alma mater mandated that prospective teacher candidates pass all segments of the Praxis series examination *before* we would be allowed to have our student teaching experience. Many colleges and universities did not require this in order to begin student teaching or graduate, but my university was different. This comprehensive assessment comprised Praxis 1 (English Language Arts, Writing, and Mathematics), Praxis 2 (Elementary Education, Secondary Education, Special Education, and School Counseling), and the PLT.

Principles of Learning and Teaching (PLT)

I had previously attempted the different sections of Praxis 1 numerous times, encountering failure each time, particularly struggling with the mathematics portion. It took me three separate tries and much assistance from my line sisters to finally conquer that specific aspect of the test. While many of my peers opted to abandon their teaching aspirations in the face of such difficulties, I refused to yield. Teaching was my passion, and I was resolute in my determination to achieve my goal.

After receiving the email notifying me that my scores were available, I closed my eyes, offered a silent prayer to God, and then opened the email. The passing score for the PLT was 161, and to my delight, my score was 168—I had passed!

This pivotal moment marked the beginning of my student-teaching journey and solidified my unwavering commitment to becoming an educator. The struggles I had faced only strengthened my resolve, proving that with determination and support, I could overcome any obstacle in pursuit of my dreams.

The surprising notification about my passing score occurred just a week before the Fall 2012 semester resumed, which was supposed to be my final semester. Because I hadn't passed the test before the spring semester ended, I was already registered with a full schedule of classes for the fall. Without hesitation, I reached out to the Director of Clinical Experiences, Evaluation, and Certification at South Carolina State University, whose office handled student teaching placements. In my call, I eagerly shared the news of my passing score from the test taken just a few weeks prior. The office assistant congratulated me and requested that I forward the email with my test results. Without wasting a moment, I swiftly sent the email, knowing that every second counted.

Anticipating a response, I eagerly awaited the next steps. True to their word, the following morning, I received an email from the assistant in Dr. O's office. Attached was a scanned copy of a letter, as my information had been received too late for a physical letter to be mailed. The letter congratulated me and confirmed our meeting time: Monday morning at eight o'clock. It provided detailed information about the class's content and also introduced the instructor.

Excited, but also curious about the dress code for this significant meeting, I reached out to a friend who was also starting student teaching. She shared that her letter contained similar information, and she advised me to dress professionally due to the rumored strictness of the instructor. It was a reminder that even in moments of celebration, preparation and professionalism were always essential.

The next week finally came around, and it was time for class. Upon entering the classroom, I was greeted by several familiar faces, including many of my sorority sisters. None of us had realized we would be embarking on this student-teaching journey together. Dr. O walked in and introduced herself, outlining the purpose of the class as well as her expectations for us as future teachers. She also provided us with our school placements for the next thirteen weeks.

My certification area was Elementary Education, so I knew my report time would be early in the morning. I questioned my ability to fulfill the student-teaching requirements because, although my placement was at the school on campus, I was not living on campus, and due to mechanical issues, I could not use my car to get there. But God made a way! Many thanks to my mom, who got up early every morning and went out of her way to take me to campus.

The day finally came, and my student teaching assignment began. I remember the excitement I felt because this was officially the start of my teaching career. It seemed as quickly as the semester began; it was over, and I had successfully completed all requirements to be inducted as a teacher in the state of South Carolina. December 10, 2012, marked my official induction.

The following semester, I was preparing for graduation and had to return to my alma mater to get a copy of a transcript. As I walked toward the building, the superintendent for the local district (who happened to be my former principal) was walking out. She asked how everything was going, and I told her I was graduating later that evening. When she asked what I majored in, I told her it was Elementary Education. She asked if I had found employment for the upcoming school year, and I told her I had not. She knew my university's policy for graduates with a degree in education and told me to stop by the district office once I finished everything at the high school. Curious, I followed her instructions.

I arrived at the district office about thirty minutes later and was directed to the office of the Director of Human Services. I walked in and was greeted by another familiar face. She congratulated me on my achievements, printed off a sheet of paper, and placed it in an envelope, which she handed to me. She advised me to celebrate my graduation, read over the document carefully, and return it if I agreed. I said, "Okay," and left the office.

Once I got in the car, I had to collect my thoughts. I opened the envelope and read it carefully. Tears of joy streamed down my face, I had officially received my first teaching contract for the upcoming school year! I was immediately reminded of **Proverbs 3:5-6 (NIV): "Trust in the LORD with all your heart and lean not on your own understanding; in all your ways submit to him, and he will make your paths straight."**

What was interesting about this situation was that I knew I *wanted* to teach, and I knew *what* I wanted to teach, but

I didn't know *where* I wanted to teach. I had to put my faith in God to send me where He knew I needed to be, and, of course, He sent me home.

Later that evening, I walked across the stage to receive my Bachelor of Science Degree in Elementary Education, graduating Magna Cum Laude. As I accepted my diploma, a flood of memories washed over me. I recalled my car accident and the doctors' grim predictions that I might never again function in a regular classroom. Yet here I was, not just functioning but excelling, ready to embark on a teaching career.

I couldn't help but think of **Philippians 4:13 (NKJV): "I can do all things through Christ who strengthens me."** This verse had been a cornerstone during my recovery and studies. It reminded me that with faith, resilience, and divine support, I could overcome any obstacle. Now, I was stepping into my future, certified and prepared to inspire and educate the next generation.

Reflection Questions

1. What early experiences in your life pointed you toward your true calling or passion?

   _____

   _____

   _____

   _____

   _____

   _____

   How have those experiences shaped your journey?

   _____

   _____

   _____

   _____

   _____

   _____

   _____

   _____

2. How did you handle moments of doubt or failure on your path to achieving your goals?

_____

_____

_____

_____

_____

_____

_____

_____

_____

What lessons did you learn from those experiences?

_____

_____

_____

_____

_____

_____

_____

_____

3. In what ways has your faith or personal belief system supported you in overcoming challenges?

_____

_____

_____

_____

_____

_____

_____

_____

Can you recall specific instances where it played a pivotal role?

_____

_____

_____

_____

_____

_____

_____

_____

_____

4. Reflect on a time when you had to rely on others for support during a difficult period.

   How did their help impact your journey, and what did you learn about the importance of community?

   _____

   _____

   _____

   _____

   _____

   _____

   _____

   _____

   _____

   _____

   _____

   _____

   _____

   _____

   _____

   _____

   _____

   _____

5. Looking back on a significant accomplishment in your life, how did overcoming past obstacles make that achievement even more meaningful?

_____

_____

_____

_____

_____

_____

_____

_____

_____

What strengths did you discover in yourself along the way?

_____

_____

_____

_____

_____

_____

_____

_____

Chapter 3

When Teaching Becomes Personal: The Student Who Taught Me Resilience

T he dawn of the 2015-2016 school year shimmered with promise, the air thick with anticipation and the scent of new beginnings. As I entered the classroom, the quiet before the storm, I couldn't shake the feeling that this year would be different. Among the sea of eager faces that would soon fill my room, one stood out—an 8-year-old girl named Jalisa, whose radiant smile and vibrant energy would quickly become the heartbeat of our class. Little did I know the inspiration and resilience I would draw from her, an unlikely source, would profoundly shape my teaching journey and my life.

August 17, 2015, marked my third "first day of school" as a third-grade teacher. I arrived at the school early that morning, eager to finalize a few tasks before my students began entering the room at 7:30 a.m. After carefully writing my name and the date on the board, I placed the freshly copied morning work on each student's desk. I prefer to let students choose their own seats on the first day, although sometimes I make a few exceptions.

As the morning progressed, students and their parents slowly filtered into the classroom. One student stood out from the rest. She wore a purple shirt with blue jeans and matching shoes. Her hair was styled in a half-up, half-down fashion, and her face beamed with the biggest smile. I had met her the previous school year and remembered that infectious smile.

"Hey, Ms. Breland," she greeted me cheerfully as she walked in.

"Hey, Jalisa," I replied, not yet realizing how integral she would become to our class. Having Jalisa in my class was like having a personal assistant with boundless enthusiasm. She had an uncanny knack for keeping everything organized and running like a well-oiled machine. From the moment she arrived, Jalisa took it upon herself to make sure every pencil was sharpened, every book was in its place, and every student was following the day's instructions. Her keen eye for detail and her gentle reminders to her classmates ensured a smoothly run classroom where everything seemed to fall into place effortlessly.

On October 11, 2015, I was at a friend's surprise birthday celebration when I received shocking news: Jalisa had been hit by a car while crossing the street to attend a high school football game. My heart sank, and I immediately picked up my phone to call her mom. Before I could press the dial button, a message from a coworker, who was also Jalisa's former teacher, confirmed the heartbreaking news and promised to keep me updated.

The night went on, and I continued to think about Jalisa. I checked Facebook for updates, and although not much information was provided, I *did* see posts about the situation. The following morning, I talked to my coworker, and she and I agreed that, with her mom's permission, we would drive up to Columbia to visit Jalisa at the hospital. Later that morning, we traveled to Columbia, which was about an hour away, eager to check on Jalisa. She was in intensive care, but we were allowed to see her. By God's grace, she had no broken bones or immediate swelling. Later, we would be informed about the injuries she had incurred.

The Monday following the accident was when the reality of Jalisa's absence truly hit me. I thought back to the last thing she said to me that Friday afternoon. Her two ponytails had been swinging as she cheerfully called out, "Bye, Ms.

Breland! See you Monday. Have a good weekend!" The thought of facing the classroom without her felt unbearable, but two factors pushed me to go to work that day. First, I knew my other students needed me, especially after hearing the tragic news. Second, finding a substitute teacher on such short notice would be difficult, and I didn't want to burden my colleagues with extra students.

I arrived at work earlier than usual, hoping to gather my thoughts before the day began. As I walked into the classroom and turned on the lights, I felt a heavy weight in my chest. Sitting at my desk, I tried to figure out how to break the news to my students when I hadn't fully processed it myself. Despite my efforts to avoid looking in that direction, my eyes were inevitably drawn to Jalisa's desk. Uncontrollable tears fell as I realized I would not see her infectious smile or hear her cheerful greetings.

The reality of not hearing her usual, "Hey, Ms. Breland" or "Y'all be quiet," and my daily, playful admonishment, "What do you want, Jalisa?" hit me hard. Overwhelmed, I left the classroom and walked across the hall to the fourth-grade math teacher's room, who happened to be my teacher-bestie. As soon as she saw me, she gave me the biggest hug, offering the comfort I desperately needed. She asked me if I felt that I would be able to stay or if I would need to go home. Then she said Jalisa was a fighter and would be okay. She also told me that my other students needed me, and I needed to be strong for them.

I eventually stopped crying and returned to my classroom. Taking a deep breath, I gathered my morning materials and began writing the daily objectives on the board. The familiar routine offered a brief moment of solace. A few minutes later, my principal walked in to check on me, her presence a quiet reassurance. Then, it was time for the students to arrive.

One by one, my students entered the classroom, their eyes reflecting the same worry and uncertainty I felt. I knew this was a conversation I had to have, but I genuinely did not want to face it. After taking attendance, I stood at the front of the room, gathering my thoughts and mustering my strength. I looked at my students and, with a voice steadier than I felt, said, "Jalisa will be okay."

The rest of the day was an adjustment, but we made it through together. In the following weeks, things gradually returned to a semblance of normalcy. I stayed in close contact with Jalisa's mom and received many positive updates about her recovery. Jalisa made miraculous progress in a short amount of time, moving from intensive care to a regular hospital room. She was then sent to a children's hospital out of state to continue her recovery and begin neurological therapy. It was initially stated that she would spend a month there... but God!

On her birthday, which was about a month after her accident, I called to wish her a happy ninth birthday. Her voice, full of excitement and hope, rang through the phone: "Ms. Breland, I'm coming home!" At that moment, I was profoundly relieved that my students were in related arts classes, giving me the privacy I needed. As soon as the call ended, tears of joy streamed down my face, a testament to the overwhelming relief and happiness I felt. This moment of emotional release was a reminder of the scripture from **Psalm 126:5 (NIV): "Those who sow with tears will reap with songs of joy."** It felt as though the tears of concern and worry we had sown were finally blossoming into the joy of her return, and I needed that quiet moment to let my emotions flow freely.

A few days later, I received the joyous news that Jalisa would be returning to school, although not until the spring semester. Given the severity of her head trauma and the many weeks of school she missed, we had to convene a meeting to determine the educational accommodations necessary for her. On December 15, 2015, the day of the meeting, I walked into the library, feeling a mix of anticipation and hope. This meeting symbolized Jalisa's return to my classroom, but I couldn't help but worry if she would remember what she'd already learned.

As I looked up, there she was—the smile I hadn't seen in almost two months, beaming back at me. My heart lifted at the sight of her. I was overwhelmed with excitement. We discussed and agreed upon all the accommodations for Jalisa, signing off on the required documents. At the conclusion of the meeting, I breathed a sigh of happiness and gave Jalisa the biggest hug ever. I asked her mom if she could stop by the classroom because I knew her friends and classmates wanted to see her. She agreed.

I hurried back to my classroom, my heart pounding with excitement, and continued the day's lessons. A few moments later, there was a knock at my door. I opened it, and Jalisa walked in. My students screamed in unison, "Jalisa!" Although I had just seen her in the meeting, something about seeing her walk through my classroom door brought indescribable happiness, hope, and relief to my heart. The room filled with joy, laughter, and the palpable sense of our little community coming back together.

The spring semester came, and Jalisa returned without missing a beat. She seamlessly slipped back into her role, reclaiming her unofficial title of teacher's assistant, which meant I was back to my daily playful refrain of "Leave me alone, Jalisa!"

I vividly remember a field trip we went on later that spring to the aquarium. As we waited to exit our classrooms to load the buses, Jalisa declared, "Ms. Breland, I'm going to sit by you." I smiled and told her she needed to find another seat partner instead. When it was time to load our class bus, another student took the seat beside me without asking. But Jalisa, ever determined, wasn't about to let that stand. With her characteristic tenacity and charm, she convinced the student to switch seats, making sure she was the one sitting next to me. As the bus rumbled toward the aquarium, Jalisa chatted animatedly, her excitement palpable. Her presence was a joyful reminder of resilience and the unbreakable bond we shared.

As the semester continued, we settled into a rhythm, finding joy in the everyday moments that followed. Jalisa eventually moved on to the next grade, but she never truly left my heart. Her presence and spirit remained a constant source of inspiration, woven into the fabric of my teaching and my life. Even now, years later, I'll occasionally receive an unexpected "Hey, Ms. Breland" text, and I know it's Jalisa, reaching out just to say hello. I often reflect on Dr. Justin Tarte's quote: "Teachers who put relationships first don't just have students for one year; they have students who view them as 'their' teacher for life." Jalisa epitomized this truth. Her journey taught me invaluable lessons about resilience and the enduring power of connections. Each time I see her smile or hear her laugh, I'm reminded of her incredible strength and the profound impact we had on each other's lives.

In the quiet moments of reflection, I realized that resilience isn't just about bouncing back; it's about growing through adversity, finding strength in the connections we forge, and embracing the journey with an open heart. Jalisa's story is a testament to the enduring power of love, support, and unwavering determination. As I moved forward, I carried with me the lessons she taught me, ready to face whatever problems the future held, knowing that in the middle of difficulty lies opportunity.

Reflection Questions

1. How has witnessing someone else's resilience (like Jalisa's) influenced your understanding of your own capacity to persevere?

_____

_____

_____

_____

_____

_____

_____

_____

_____

_____

_____

_____

_____

_____

_____

_____

2. In what ways have relationships in your life, whether personal or professional, reinforced your ability to navigate challenges?

_____

_____

_____

_____

_____

_____

_____

_____

_____

_____

_____

_____

_____

_____

_____

_____

_____

_____

_____

3. How do you define resilience when faced with unexpected difficulties?

_____

_____

_____

_____

_____

_____

_____

_____

_____

Has this definition changed over time? If so, how?

_____

_____

_____

_____

_____

_____

_____

_____

_____

4. Think about a time when someone in your life impacted you deeply.

How did that experience shape your perspective on the importance of connection and support?

_____

_____

_____

_____

_____

_____

_____

_____

_____

_____

_____

_____

_____

_____

_____

_____

_____

5. What emotions or thoughts come to mind when you reflect on the significant relationships in your life?

_____

_____

_____

_____

_____

_____

_____

_____

How do these connections influence how you approach challenges?

_____

_____

_____

_____

_____

_____

_____

_____

_____

Chapter 4

Echoes of Fragility: Confronting Life's Unpredictability

In a sterile room, where the scent of antiseptic hung heavy in the air and the fluorescent lights cast a cold, unyielding glow, my world shifted. The rhythmic beeping of monitors punctuated the quiet urgency of the space, blending with the soft murmur of medical professionals. Every sound, every scent, every sensation felt magnified as I lay there, my heart pounding with a mix of fear and determination. The journey to the hospital had been just the beginning. Now, I stood at the threshold of an entirely different kind of journey, one that demanded not just courage, but an unyielding resilience and a profound will to survive. As I looked around the room, the reality of my situation settled in, and I knew this was a battle I had to face head-on.

* * *

Let's rewind to the beginning. The 2016-2017 school year brought a significant change: I accepted a new teaching position in a new school district. Although it was my fourth year of teaching, stepping into a new grade level and environment made me feel like a first-year teacher again. Just when I had become comfortable with my teaching ability, here I was—at the beginning again. All my expertise, thus far, had been with early elementary school students; now, I was stepping into upper elementary territory. This would be a whole new world, so I immersed myself in studying the content and readjusting my teaching skills, gradually building my confidence.

Then came mid-November. After wrapping up a math lesson, I was grading papers at my desk when a student raised their hand for help. As I stood up, a sharp, throbbing pain shot through my foot, so intense that it felt like a hot iron stabbing through my flesh. I could hardly lift it. After a few painful moments, I was able to brush it off and assist the student, but by the end of the day, I could barely walk and had to roll across my classroom floor using a chair. At home, I tried to nurse my foot, but the pain persisted. Because it wasn't swollen, I assumed it wasn't broken or sprained, so I avoided urgent care and instead scheduled an appointment with a podiatrist.

A few days later, the podiatrist's x-ray confirmed my foot was not sprained or broken. Instead, a dark shadow on the film revealed the true culprit: a mass on a muscle in my foot, causing excruciating pain. The doctor's words were clear: surgery was the only solution. My mind raced back to the spring of 2008 when I had postponed foot surgery because it would have required using a wheelchair during my first weeks of college. Who wanted to start their college experience in a wheelchair if they could help it? It seemed fate had a funny way of catching up with me, but this time, I couldn't avoid it.

The surgery was scheduled for December 9, 2016. As the day approached, my anxiety swelled, my mind racing with a thousand *what-ifs*. Although this would be my second medical procedure, this would be the first time I was conscious enough to consider the possible risks. Nights were restless, filled with visions of the operating room and the unknowns that lay ahead. On the morning of the surgery, my stomach churned with a mixture of fear and hope, every second feeling like an eternity. It seemed like a never-ending drive as my big sister drove me to the hospital. Yet, despite my trepidation, everything went as planned. The surgery was successful, but the real test was just beginning.

Post-surgery, I was ordered to strictly limit activity on my leg. The initial days of recovery were grueling. Confined to bed, I was enveloped in a haze of painkillers, anti-nausea medication, and sleep. The room around me morphed into a blur of indistinguishable shapes and sounds. Each day was a battle against discomfort and restlessness, the boundaries of my world shrinking to the four walls of my bedroom.

Slowly, I began to move around with the help of crutches. Each step was a monumental effort, a careful balancing act that sent jolts of pain through my leg. The once simple act of walking had transformed into a painstaking ordeal, every movement a stark reminder of the trauma my body had endured. The crutches dug into my arms, and the floor felt like shifting sand beneath my feet. Each shuffle forward was a triumph over adversity, a testament to my determination to heal and reclaim my mobility.

At my first post-op check-up, the doctor replaced my cumbersome cast with a medical boot, a small victory that gave me a semblance of mobility. With the boot in place, I was cleared to return to work, a decision that brought both relief and trepidation. Unfortunately, the return was short-lived; my body needed more time to heal, and I was sent home to fully recuperate.

One night, as I lay in bed, attempting to rest, a peculiar sensation coursed through my leg. Despite being still, my leg felt restless and agitated from within, as if something inside was throbbing and pulsing with an unnatural rhythm. The next morning, I woke to a horrifying sight—my leg had swollen to twice its normal size! It was warm to the touch and throbbing with pain. Panic set in as I contacted my mom and described the alarming symptoms. "You need to call your doctor immediately," she urged.

Taking her advice, I reached out to my doctor. Hearing the urgency in my voice, she rearranged her schedule and instructed me to meet her at the hospital's vein clinic immediately. My heart raced as I prepared to leave, anxiety gnawing at me with every step. The short journey to the clinic felt interminable, the pain in my leg intensifying with each passing moment.

With my heart pounding and my leg aching, I arrived at the clinic within the hour. The scans revealed a large blood clot, known as Deep Vein Thrombosis (DVT), stretching from my ankle nearly to my knee. DVT is a serious condition where a blood clot forms in a deep vein, often in the leg, causing swelling and pain. If left untreated, the clot can break loose and travel to the lungs, leading to a potentially life-threatening situation called a "pulmonary embolism."

The severity of the situation hit me like a ton of bricks as I was wheeled into the emergency room. A swirl of emotions—fear, frustration, and uncertainty—washed over me. I called my mom, my voice trembling as I said, "I have a blood clot." The words sounded surreal even to my own ears, making the reality of my condition even more daunting.

Despite the gravity of my condition, the emergency room was a lesson in patience. Hours crawled by before a doctor finally examined me. I was prescribed Eliquis, a newer blood thinner, and instructed to go home. Insurance complications meant hospitalization wasn't an option, adding another layer of complexity to an already overwhelming situation. As I left the hospital, a sense of fragile hope mingled with the reality of my precarious health, knowing that the journey to recovery was far from over.

Following discharge instructions, I had a check-up with my primary care doctor and was cleared to return to work. On the way home, my chest started to hurt, a sharp and alarming pain that grew worse with each breath. My mom, sensing the urgency, quickly drove me to the hospital. Recognizing the severity, the hospital staff expedited my admission. Blood work and an EKG were normal, but a CT scan with contrast revealed the culprit: a pulmonary embolism. I was admitted immediately.

The first few days in the hospital were a jarring adjustment. The regimented schedule was relentless: frequent blood pressure checks that interrupted my sleep, blood work at all hours that left my arms bruised and sore, daily blood thinner injections that stung with each dose, constant doctor visits that blurred together, and rigidly scheduled mealtimes that felt out of sync with my appetite.

Despite these treatments, my blood levels swung wildly. If they were too high, I faced the terrifying risk of severe bleeding; if too low, the ever-present danger of more clots loomed ominously. For ten excruciating days, I endured this frustrating cycle, each day blending into the next in a haze of anxiety and exhaustion. The hospital room became my world, a place where time seemed to stand still, punctuated only by the beeping of monitors and the quiet murmur of medical staff.

One morning, after yet another tearful breakdown caused by the relentless pain of my IV site and the frustration of my new "normal," a young travel nurse noticed my distress. It had been a week since I had last taken a shower because I couldn't get that area wet, and the discomfort was unbearable. With a compassionate smile, she promised to help me feel better. Returning with a plastic bag to cover the area, she gently secured it in place and encouraged me to take a shower. That small act of kindness made a significant difference, offering a moment of normalcy and relief in an otherwise bleak environment. After the shower, I felt a wave of refreshment wash over me.

The day before, my younger cousin Chelsea had come to visit. Seeing my disheveled state, she had taken the time to detangle and braid my hair, a task I couldn't manage due to the pain in my arm from the IV. Her loving care and the nurse's thoughtful gesture made me feel human again, lifting my spirits in a way that medical treatments alone could not. I also received countless text messages from Jalisa, asking if I was okay, checking for updates on my release, and encouraging comments about how she would be happy to miss school to come keep me company.

A few days later, I was discharged from the hospital, but not out of danger. The blood clot in my leg hadn't fully dissolved, leading to a complex and strict medication routine. My doctor prescribed a new blood thinner, Xarelto, hoping it would be the solution, but within days, I began to break out in hives all over my face and neck. The itching and swelling were unbearable, and I felt like my body was betraying me. Alarmed, my doctor called me in immediately. Her eyes widened in shock as she examined my swollen, blotchy skin. "Oh, my goodness, I think we've made it worse," she exclaimed, her voice laced with concern. This forced her to revert to Warfarin, a more reliable, older medication.

It's funny how we come up with new ways to try to fix old issues when the old ways still get the job done. The older medication didn't cause any allergic reactions, but it required careful monitoring. Weekly blood tests and frequent scans became my new normal, each appointment a reminder of the precarious balance my health now required. Each visit to the clinic was a journey of hope and anxiety, knowing that maintaining this delicate equilibrium was essential for my survival. The experience taught me a profound lesson in resilience and adaptability, underscoring the importance of tried-and-true methods in a world constantly chasing innovation.

As summer approached, life continued to try my resilience in ways I hadn't anticipated. I remember heading to the 53rd National Convention of Delta Sigma Theta Sorority, Incorporated, in Las Vegas, Nevada, on August 2, 2017. Even with my recent medical concerns, as alumnae chapter president, I was expected to attend. The excitement of the trip was overshadowed by a gnawing anxiety. On the way to the airport, my doctor called with urgent news: my blood was as "thin as water." She suggested I cancel the trip, but I was already en route and just minutes away from the airport, which was two hours from home. Her voice was filled with concern as she warned me to be extremely careful and to get my blood checked as soon as I arrived in Las Vegas. My heart sank, but I knew I had to push forward.

The journey to Las Vegas became a blur of caution and constant self-monitoring. Every step felt like walking on a tightrope, the fear of the slightest injury looming over me. On the flight to the convention, I accidentally hit my arm on the armrest and was left with a distinctly noticeable, hideous, purple bruise on my arm. Other chapter members who were traveling with me became fearful and urged me to be extra careful.

Once we landed, I took a picture of the bruise and texted it to my doctor. As soon as she received the picture, she called me. She told me to monitor the bruise and make sure it didn't change color or start to give off heat. If it did, she instructed me to get to the nearest emergency room right away.

I was afraid, knowing I was in another state, far from my family and doctors who didn't know me or my medical history. Before we ended the call, my doctor attempted a bit of dry humor, adding, "Try not to do anything else."

At the conference, I found it hard to focus on the sessions because my mind was preoccupied with the precarious state of my health. The bustling city and the lively atmosphere felt distant as I navigated my own private storm of worry and vigilance. It was difficult to enjoy my time away, engage freely with others, or simply relax between sessions. I returned home on August 11th, marking the most extended stay I had ever had in Las Vegas.

Back in the classroom teaching, I tried to regain a sense of normalcy. Then, one Sunday morning, about a month after my return, I went to church, seeking solace and peace. But as fate would have it, I stumbled and fell. The moment I hit the ground, panic set in. I had fallen on my knee, which resulted in a deep scrape. Blood began to pour from the wound, and it wouldn't stop. The relentless bleeding was a stark reminder of the blood thinners coursing through my veins. My heart raced as I was rushed back to the hospital for treatment. The doctors worked quickly to stop the bleeding, but the incident left me shaken.

Being on blood thinners meant I bruised at the slightest touch. Something as simple as someone grabbing my arm could leave me with dark purple bruises, a painful reminder of my vulnerability. Each bruise felt like a badge of the battle I was fighting, visible marks of the invisible struggle within my body.

The constant cycle of fear, caution, and medical emergencies tested my strength daily. Despite these struggles, I clung to hope and the determination to reclaim my life. Every day was a fight to maintain a sense of normalcy and to push through the physical and emotional pain that threatened to overwhelm me. The journey was arduous, but each step forward, no matter how small, was a victory in itself.

It was nearly two years before I was officially cleared of all blood clots. I remember that day vividly, as if it were yesterday. My vascular specialist performed the scans as usual and came into the room to explain the findings. His face lit up with a reassuring smile as he told me that although my leg continued to swell, there were no new blood clots, and the one they had been monitoring had finally dissolved. Relief washed over me, and I felt like the woman with the issue of blood from the story told in Mark 5:25-34. She had suffered constant bleeding for twelve years but kept her faith and was finally healed when she touched the hem of Jesus' garment.

At that moment, I truly understood the depth of her faith and her determination to seek healing despite years of suffering. Her story resonated deeply with me, as I, too, had faced a long, arduous journey filled with pain, uncertainty, and moments of despair. But like her, I had clung to hope and perseverance. The relief and joy I felt were indescribable, a testament to the power of resilience and faith.

This experience taught me a profound lesson: that true healing often requires unwavering faith and the strength to endure, no matter how difficult the journey. In the face of relentless adversity, I discovered an inner resilience I never knew I had. The support of my family, the dedication of my medical team, and my unwavering faith were my anchors. Every bruise, every injection, and every hospital visit became part of a story of survival and perseverance.

As I reflect on this chapter of my life, I realize it was more than a battle against illness; it was a journey of self-discovery and growth. I learned that resilience isn't about never facing difficulties; it's about how you confront them and find strength in moments of weakness. Each experience taught me to appreciate the small victories and to hold on to hope, even when the path ahead seemed uncertain.

This experience has forever changed me, instilling in me a deeper appreciation for life and the people who stood by me. It taught me that healing is not just a physical process but an emotional and spiritual one as well. As I close this chapter, I do so with gratitude for the lessons learned and the strength gained. The journey continues, but I face it now with a renewed spirit and an unshakable faith in my ability to overcome whatever lies ahead.

Reflection Questions

1. What challenges have you faced in your life that tested your resilience?

_____

_____

_____

_____

_____

_____

_____

_____

_____

_____

_____

_____

_____

_____

_____

_____

_____

_____

_____

2. Reflect on a time when you encountered a significant obstacle.

    How did you respond, and what did you learn about your own strength and capacity for perseverance?

    _____

    _____

    _____

    _____

    _____

    _____

    _____

    _____

    _____

    _____

    _____

    _____

    _____

    _____

    _____

    _____

    _____

    _____

3. How do you find hope and strength during difficult times?

_____

_____

_____

_____

_____

_____

_____

_____

_____

_____

_____

_____

_____

_____

_____

_____

_____

_____

_____

_____

4. Think about the sources of support and encouragement in your life.

How do they help you maintain hope and motivation when facing challenges?

_____

_____

_____

_____

_____

_____

_____

_____

_____

_____

_____

_____

_____

_____

_____

_____

_____

5. What small victories have you celebrated on your journey of overcoming adversity?

_____

_____

_____

_____

_____

_____

_____

Consider the minor achievements that have marked your progress.

How do these small wins contribute to your overall sense of accomplishment and resilience?

_____

_____

_____

_____

_____

_____

_____

_____

_____

6. In what ways can you apply the lessons of resilience and perseverance to your current life situations?

_____

_____

_____

_____

_____

_____

_____

_____

_____

_____

_____

_____

_____

_____

_____

_____

_____

7. Identify areas in your life where you can draw upon the strength and resilience you have developed.

_____

_____

_____

_____

_____

_____

_____

_____

How can these lessons help you navigate future challenges?

_____

_____

_____

_____

_____

_____

_____

_____

8. How has your journey of overcoming challenges shaped your perspective on life and your relationships with others?

_____

_____

_____

_____

_____

_____

_____

_____

_____

_____

_____

_____

_____

_____

_____

_____

_____

_____

_____

_____

9. Reflect on how your experiences have influenced your appreciation for life and the people around you.

How have these experiences strengthened your connections and understanding of others?

_____

_____

_____

_____

_____

_____

_____

_____

_____

_____

_____

_____

_____

_____

_____

_____

_____

_____

10. What practices or habits help you maintain emotional and spiritual well-being during challenging times?

_____

_____

_____

_____

_____

_____

_____

List strategies you use to cope with stress and maintain balance.

_____

_____

_____

_____

_____

How can these practices support you in continuing to build resilience and emotional health?

_____

_____

_____

_____

_____

Chapter 5

From Closure to Connection: Teaching Beyond Classroom Walls

The spring of 2020 brought an unexpected twist to my teaching journey. As the school year approached its end, none of us could have predicted the abrupt halt that awaited us. The looming shadow of the COVID-19 pandemic abruptly disrupted the familiar rhythms of classroom chatter, students' laughter, and the comforting routine of lesson plans.

Friday, March 13, 2020, started like any other day. I reviewed my math lesson on multiplying fractions and told my students that on Monday, we would begin learning how to divide fractions. News had begun airing about a deadly "virus," but many South Carolinians felt relatively safe since we had no confirmed cases.

As the bell rang and school was dismissed, our principal scheduled an informal faculty meeting to discuss emergency plans. Since it was a Friday meeting, we expected it to be quick. She informed us that the district had asked schools to prepare plans for a potential closure but emphasized there was no immediate rush. She asked us to prepare a packet of materials to distribute to students in the event of a closure, giving us until the following week to get it ready. After the meeting, we went home, unaware of the imminent changes.

Saturday, March 14, 2020, unfolded like any other weekend. I spent the day recuperating from a week of teaching and ran around completing errands I could only get to on the weekend. On Sunday, March 15th, I went to church in the morning as usual. A little after 4:00 p.m., word began to spread that the governor of South Carolina would give a briefing about the state's plan for handling COVID-19.

That evening, on national television, the governor announced the decision to close *all* schools through the end of the month. My fifth-grade team and I were in a group text, all sharing the same initial reaction of shock and disbelief. A few minutes later, our principal messaged us, stating that while she was also surprised by information disclosed during the briefing, we would still report to the building the next day. This day would be solely dedicated to preparing materials for students, which would then be distributed on Wednesday because of the governor's sudden decision. As I was only responsible for teaching math, I started brainstorming review work that would be engaging and not too repetitive.

All day Monday and part of Tuesday, we worked tirelessly to gather and copy materials for our students. By Wednesday, tables were set up in the carpool area of the school for each grade level. Parents and students came to the designated tables to pick up their packets. Each homeroom teacher had a sign-out sheet and was available to answer any questions parents had.

After we were dismissed for the day, our principal informed us that she would keep us updated on how to proceed with the school year and would relay any further directions from the district. While many appreciated the unexpected pause from the daily hustle and bustle of teaching, I quickly began to miss my students. I used ClassDojo to communicate with parents, held weekly check-ins with my students over Zoom, and mailed birthday cards to those who celebrated while we were out.

The next few weeks were filled with uncertainty and disbelief. The initial closure for March was extended through April and eventually for the rest of the school year. My school held two more packet distribution days to help finish the year.

On the last day of school, we organized a farewell parade. Each grade level decorated tables along the carpool lane, and families drove through with posters, banners, and signs as students said goodbye to the teachers.

The remainder of that spring and summer would prove to be equally challenging. Amid the extended shutdown, mask mandates, and limited medical assistance, I would face a personal health scare that would test my strength like never before. Adding to the stress, I would also learn that my cousin was involved in a near-fatal car accident. Later that summer, I would lose four family members, two passing away on the same day from COVID-19. Because of the pandemic and medical concerns of close relatives, I would not be able to attend any of their funeral services.

Finally, August rolled around, and it was time for back-to-school preparations. This time, back-to-school had an entirely new look. Instead of meeting my students at a traditional open house, I met them through Google Meet. The upside to this school year was that I didn't have to spend hours of the day or weekends at school getting my classroom ready for students. I was one of two virtual teachers for my grade level, so all my instruction would take place online. On the first day of school, I was assigned twenty-three new fifth-graders.

I had to get creative with how I would instruct this group of students, especially since I had never taught online before, and the Learning Management System (LMS) we were using was entirely new to me. The first few days were an adjustment, filled with hours of technical difficulties while both my students and I learned to navigate this new style of teaching and learning.

Initially, our virtual classroom was plagued with dropped connections, frozen screens, and confusing log-ins. It was a steep learning curve for all of us. However, through perseverance and patience, I finally developed a routine, worked out all the bugs, and created a smooth-running virtual classroom. My days began with posting the daily agenda, followed by live lessons and interactive activities. I incorporated videos, quizzes, and group work through breakout rooms, making sure every student was engaged and learning.

One morning, after the first lesson of the day, I asked if any students had questions. One student raised his hand and innocently asked, "Ms. Breland, can I please go to the restroom?" I couldn't help but laugh at how endearing and interesting the question was—he was in his own home, yet still felt the need to ask for permission. "Of course you can!" I responded with a smile, appreciating the small moment that highlighted the unique blend of home and school life we were navigating together.

These brief moments underscored the adaptability and resilience we were all learning to embrace. My students were not just learning academic lessons; they were also learning life lessons in flexibility and perseverance, and I was right there with them, adapting and growing every day.

Virtual teaching gave me a new perspective on the home lives of my students and how school served as a safe haven for many of them. I remember one student who had to go into the closet of her room just to find a quiet environment for learning. She would log in each day from her makeshift study space, her determination shining through despite the struggle. "I just want to be able to hear you, Ms. Breland," she would say, her voice filled with both resolve and vulnerability.

Another student craved connection in this time of isolation. She often lingered after our virtual class sessions ended, seeking to spend more time with her classmates and me. "Can we stay a little longer?" she would ask, her eyes reflecting the loneliness that many children felt during the pandemic. She found comfort in our online classroom, where she could interact and feel a sense of normalcy.

My virtual learning schedule consisted of designated instructional times for English Language Arts/Reading (ELA/R), Mathematics, and an alternating schedule for Science and Social Studies. Each morning, I posted the daily agenda, and at the designated time, I began instruction. The day started with ELA/R, followed by math, then a break for lunch, and concluded with a science or social studies lesson. I followed the Gradual Release of Responsibility Framework for learning, which is broken down into three parts: *I Do* (direct teaching/modeling), *We Do* (guided practice), and *You Do* (independent practice). During guided practice, I either did whole group practice or split the class into breakout rooms where they could collaborate on a skill or problem, and I would join different rooms to guide as needed. For independent practice, I stayed on Google Meet with my camera off. If a student had a question, I could quickly respond by turning my camera on.

In the beginning, most students stayed on until they finished their independent work, but over time, they left the meeting and rejoined if they had questions. One day, after weeks of following this routine and a morning of technical difficulties that made me question if virtual instruction was for me, one of my students rejoined the Google Meet, not because she was confused, but just because she wanted to check on me. She asked how I was doing and stayed online with me for over an hour. During that time, she taught me how to play her favorite board game, *Guess Who?* She also shared some notes from a church service she attended, titled "Living in Victory," and gave me a virtual tour of her home.

This experience reminded me of a lesson taken from **Galatians 6:2 (NIV): "Carry each other's burdens, and in this way you will fulfill the law of Christ."** Amid challenges and uncertainty, my student showed empathy and care, offering support when I needed it most. Her kindness was a powerful reminder that we are all called to help and uplift one another, especially during difficult times.

The end of the first nine weeks was approaching, and the decision to remain virtual or transition to face-to-face instruction loomed large. Teaching in a classroom was what I was accustomed to and more prepared for, but although some parents chose to send their children back to a traditional school, I didn't want to abandon the virtual students I'd grown to love over the last nine weeks. As a teacher, the end of the school year is always bittersweet, knowing my students will move on to the next grade, school, or stage in life. Surprisingly, this same sentiment emerged at the end of that first nine-week period.

If I decided to teach face-to-face, I would continue with some of my original students, but new students would also be assigned to me. While I could bond with any student and establish a routine, I didn't want to start over with teaching class procedures as well. So, I made the decision to face a new beast and voluntarily become a hybrid teacher. This meant I would continue teaching my virtual students online while also instructing those returning to in-person learning. Although it sounded straightforward because these students already knew me and my expectations, transitioning from completely virtual to hybrid was daunting. On top of that, I had to ensure my classroom adhered to COVID-19 guidelines: desks spaced apart, plexiglass shields on desks, proper disinfecting, no sharing of items, no physical contact, and accurately reporting any students showing signs of illness. These were my responsibilities—all this while still instructing students, both virtually and in person.

Teaching at a Title I school presented unique setbacks, especially as it pertained to ensuring all students had access to necessary supplies. Many families struggled to afford basic items, making it crucial for me to bridge the gap between my virtual and in-person students. This meant countless late nights and long weekends spent converting paper copies into digital files. Often, I found myself making personal purchases and delivering items to my students' homes to ensure they had what they needed. Despite these difficulties, I was determined to make it work. As the school year drew to a close, I faced the bittersweet task of saying congratulations and goodbye to both my virtual and in-person students. I vividly remember the last daily agenda slide I posted for them, displayed in bright, cheerful colors, with a simple yet heartfelt message: "I love you all. Class dismissed."

As we prepared for the next school year, which was set to be entirely in-person with occasional virtual days, we couldn't have anticipated the lasting impact virtual instruction would have on public education. The transition was tough, and the effects of our pandemic-era teaching methods lingered, influencing everything from classroom dynamics to student engagement.

Reflecting on this experience, I recall the verse from **Galatians 6:9 (NIV): "Let us not become weary in doing good, for at the proper time we will reap a harvest if we do not give up."** The year was challenging, but it taught me the value of perseverance and the profound impact a dedicated teacher can have on their students, even in the most trying of times.

Resilience became my constant companion during this time. Every day brought new challenges, but I adapted and persevered, ensuring my students continued to learn and feel supported. The pandemic tested my strength and dedication but also reinforced my commitment to my students and to the teaching profession.

As I closed this chapter, I carried with me the lessons learned from a year like no other. The pandemic disrupted our world, but it also revealed our extraordinary capacity to adapt, support one another, and continue moving forward. True resilience is born not from the circumstances we encounter but from our ability to adapt, persevere, and find strength within ourselves and each other. With these insights, I was ready to face whatever obstacles the future held, knowing I could overcome anything.

Reflection Questions

1. How did the sudden changes brought on by the pandemic impact your ability to adapt to new situations, personally or professionally?

_____

_____

_____

_____

_____

_____

Reflect on your initial reactions to the abrupt changes in your everyday environment and note how you managed to overcome the challenges.

_____

_____

_____

_____

_____

_____

_____

2. In what ways did the pandemic challenge your resilience, and how did you find strength during those times?

    _____

    _____

    _____

    _____

    _____

    _____

    _____

    _____

    Consider the personal and professional obstacles you faced and note the strategies you used to maintain your resilience.

    _____

    _____

    _____

    _____

    _____

    _____

    _____

    _____

    _____

3. What role did empathy and compassion play in your interactions with others (colleagues, clients, or family members) during this period?

_____

_____

_____

_____

_____

_____

_____

Think about how emotional connections with others influenced your approach to interacting with others and how you supported one another.

_____

_____

_____

_____

_____

_____

_____

_____

4. How did this experience reshape your perspective on the importance of flexibility in your profession and your life?

_____

_____

_____

_____

_____

_____

_____

_____

Reflect on how adapting to new work methods and environments has influenced your views on flexibility and its role in overcoming adversity.

_____

_____

_____

_____

_____

_____

_____

_____

5. How can the lessons you learned during this challenging time be applied to future obstacles you may encounter?

_____

_____

_____

_____

_____

_____

_____

_____

Consider the broader implications of the resilience you developed. How can it serve you in other aspects of your personal and/or professional life?

_____

_____

_____

_____

_____

_____

_____

_____

Chapter 6

Holding On to Hope: Trusting God's Report

L ife has a way of throwing the unexpected at us… when we *least* expect it! A single phone call can turn a routine day into a whirlwind of fear, uncertainty, and—ultimately resilience. My world was irrevocably changed by such a call—one that plunged me into a story of survival against all odds and taught me more about courage and strength than I ever imagined possible.

The Day Everything Changed

Thursday, May 7, 2020, began like any other day, even though we were in the midst of a pandemic. I had just returned from a 7:00 a.m. shopping trip. With many businesses either shut down or altering their hours, I had made a habit of shopping early, often being the first customer to walk through Walmart's doors. The store was eerily quiet, the shelves still freshly stocked. The emptiness of the aisles was a stark contrast to the chaos outside, but it was a small comfort amidst the uncertainty of the pandemic.

Once I arrived home, I unpacked and put away my groceries, and then my phone rang. It was my mom, her voice carrying an unusual edge.

"Francena said to pray for Chelsea. She's been in an accident and is at the hospital."

My heart skipped a beat, but my mom's tone didn't suggest immediate alarm.

"I hope she's okay," I replied, trying to keep my voice steady. We exchanged a few more words before hanging up, leaving me with a sense of unease that I tried to shake off.

An hour later, the phone rang again. This time, my mom's voice was different—urgent, fraught with fear. "I just spoke to Pit. It's not good," she said, her words tumbling out in a rush. She was referring to my Uncle Pit, Aunt Francena's husband and Chelsea's father. We were on a four-way call with my aunt Leah and cousin Amanda, and the gravity of the situation quickly sank in.

"I'm leaving work early. We need to get to the hospital as quickly as we can," my mom instructed.

We lived about an hour from the hospital they had transported Chelsea to, but we knew we needed to get there ASAP. My mom, Aunt Leah, Amanda, and I quickly gathered at my house and then hopped into the car. As I sped off toward Augusta, Georgia, my mom called my brother to tell him what was going on, and he said he would meet us at the hospital. Aunt Leah also called her husband, my Uncle Larry, and he said he would meet us there as well.

Panic began to set in. My mind raced with questions and worst-case scenarios. The normalcy of the morning had dissolved into a fog of anxiety and dread. The car ride to the hospital, which took an hour, felt endless, with each moment stretching into an eternity as I gripped the steering wheel, my knuckles white with tension. The world outside the car windows rushed past, my focus entirely on the road ahead and the fear knotting in my stomach. The drive felt like a race against time, each mile stretching our nerves tighter. My mind was a whirlwind of worry and fear, every passing minute amplifying the urgency of our mission. The usually scenic route to Georgia blurred past us, the trees and buildings merging into a dizzying backdrop of anxiety.

We finally reached the hospital, parked the car hastily, and called my Aunt Francena to inform her of our arrival. My mom, hearing the distress in her younger sister's voice, knew she had to find her quickly. As we approached the hospital's entrance, it loomed ahead like a gateway to unknown outcomes and fragile hopes. Unfortunately, due to COVID-19 restrictions, we were not allowed to go inside. That realization hit us hard; we would have to wait outside, unsure of what was happening within the hospital walls.

Aunt Francena walked toward us and immediately broke down in tears. I had always known my aunt to be this invincible person; growing up, I couldn't recall ever seeing her cry. She was the rock of our family, the epitome of strength and resilience. I remember writing school papers about my aunt being my hero because of her unwavering fortitude during adversity, but this time, I knew she had been as strong as she could be, and she needed support. Seeing her hurt broke me, and that's when it truly hit me how serious my cousin's condition was. The weight of the situation settled heavily on my shoulders, pressing down with a relentless force.

By this time, my brother (who lived about two hours away) and Uncle Larry had arrived. We gathered outside the hospital, each of us trying to process the gravity of the situation while adhering to the COVID-19 restrictions that kept us from entering. The hours dragged on painfully as we waited for updates. Aunt Francena received phone calls about Chelsea's condition and was eventually informed that she was out of surgery and in the trauma unit. The relief was fleeting, overtaken quickly by ongoing unease as we continued to wait.

We spent the entire afternoon and much of the evening outside, the hours dragging by painfully slowly. The atmosphere was heavy with the weight of our worries, the sterile scent of disinfectant occasionally wafting out whenever the hospital doors opened. Waiting outside the hospital felt surreal, every sound and movement amplified by our worry.

The sight of my family gathered together, their faces etched with worry, was a punch to the gut. We huddled in the parking lot, a collective force of hope and prayer, waiting for news about Chelsea's condition. The tension was unbearable, each of us clinging to any shred of hope we could find. The waiting area outside became our temporary refuge, filled with anxious energy as we desperately sought updates and comforted one another.

Eventually, we were allowed to enter the hospital to see Chelsea, but only one person at a time. My Uncle Pit went first, followed by Aunt Francena. When she walked out from seeing her daughter, her physical and emotional appearance had changed, the weight of the situation etched deeply into her face.

Then it was my turn. I walked to the tent where hospital staff were conducting screenings because of several confirmed cases of COVID-19 at the hospital. After having my temperature checked, the nurses cleared me, gave me a new mask, and directed me on how to get to my cousin's location. As I stepped off the elevator and got closer to the trauma unit doors, my heart began pounding, and my eyes watered. Being in a trauma unit was something I should have been used to, but this time, it was not. I knew what everyone said to expect, but I still did not want to accept it.

I've always heard the phrase that your cousins are your first best friends. I momentarily lost myself in memories of the days Chelsea, Amanda, and I spent playing together at my grandma's house. We'd done almost everything together, even getting in trouble together, so it was hard to imagine something happening to one of us. Reality set back in quickly. I was the older cousin, and I did not want to see my best friend, my younger cousin, in a hospital bed connected to all this medical equipment. I walked through the doors, turned the corner, and my heart sank. I looked at the girl lying in the bed, and although the name on the door was Chelsea's, I could not accept that this was my cousin. This was *not* Chelsea—definitely not the same cousin who had visited me every time I was in the hospital—the one who did my hair for me while I was sick and unable to do it for myself. This wasn't my "Little Big Dawg" (my nickname for her because although I was older, she was a little taller and more adventurous than I was), and in that moment, I couldn't be her "Big Little Dawg." This was *not* my cousin.

I looked down at her nails. One thing about Chelsea was that she always kept her nails and hair done. She always wore her nails uniquely designed and extremely long, but now they had been cut. Her hair had been shaved, and her head was bandaged from surgery. I looked at her face, but it was so swollen that she didn't look like herself. And although her eyes were open, she wasn't moving. A machine was breathing for her. I finally looked at her arm. Chelsea had several tattoos, and although the tattoos signaled it was her, I still could not accept it. Time stood still, and I froze.

I rubbed her arm and found she was warm. To maintain my sanity, I've always been one who would laugh to keep from crying, so I told her not to make any sudden movements or else I'd end up in a bed next to her. I never took my hand off her the entire time I was there. While holding her hand and rubbing her arm, I said, "Chelsea, it's supposed to be me. *You* come to visit *me* in the hospital. This is not right." I felt like I was going to break down, so I had another moment of having to laugh to keep from crying. Because she also had surgery on her head, I told her that others would know we were related because now we would have matching scars. Mine goes from my forehead around to the front of my right ear, while hers looks like a headband going from the left side of her head to the right.

I talked to her for a little while longer and then said a prayer before I physically left that room. It felt as if, although I was walking away, a part of me stayed in that room with Chelsea. I walked back outside and waited for the last person to come back from seeing her. Eventually, everyone left, and we went our separate ways.

I drove home with my mom beside me, her voice steady but filled with concern as she updated family members over the phone. The car felt heavy with unspoken emotions, and I struggled to name what I was feeling—was it worry, anger, relief, or some tangled mix of all three? A part of me felt a quiet relief that she was still here, still fighting. But another part of me was consumed by worry, imagining what might come next.

Although focused on the road ahead, my mind was somewhere else. I pleaded with God to keep Chelsea here, to lay His healing hands upon her body and restore her strength. In those moments of uncertainty and hope, my growing understanding of resilience and faith became my anchor—a guiding light that steadied me through the darkness with unwavering resolve.

Miracles in the Midst of Despair

That Sunday, which happened to be Mother's Day (ironically, the same day I had my first car accident years ago), brought devastating news: Chelsea had suffered a stroke on the right side of her brain, affecting the left side of her body. It really seems true that when it rains, it pours. Later, the doctors told us they had done all they could do and didn't think she would make it. I remember my aunt later sharing that when they were given that heartbreaking news, my uncle told the doctor, "You're a man, and you've done all you can do, but God hasn't done all He can do. I'm going to keep my faith."

My pastor, Dr. Dharius Daniels, once said, "A miracle is a divinely orchestrated anomaly and aberration. It's when God makes something happen that shouldn't happen, couldn't happen, and wouldn't happen unless He made it happen." At that moment, I needed a miracle. I needed God to make her open her eyes, get out of that bed, and stop playing this cruel game with me. As much of a fixer as I try to be, I knew I couldn't fix her, so I did the next best thing. I went into prayer and prayed for God to heal Chelsea as only He could.

I called my cousin Amanda and tried to relay what my aunt had told us, but I couldn't get the words out through my tears, only managing to say the first few words before breaking down completely. I had always heard people speak of feeling their heart break, but this time, I truly understood what that meant. The pain was overwhelming. To make matters worse, Chelsea also had a seizure and needed another surgery to insert a shunt into her head.

Time passed, and Chelsea gradually showed signs of responsiveness. In June, the doctors recommended moving her to a rehabilitation hospital in Atlanta, Georgia, where she could receive more specialized care. Given the distance and the specific medical attention Chelsea needed, my aunt made the difficult decision to take early retirement and accompany her to Atlanta. On June 19, 2020, Chelsea was transferred to the rehab hospital. During her stay, she underwent a medical procedure to replace a bone in her head that had been removed during her initial surgery. She remained at the rehabilitation hospital for three months before finally being released to go home. God was answering our prayers!

Initially, we refrained from visiting her at her home because of the ongoing pandemic and the risk of infection. A few weeks passed, and one Sunday, we decided it was time to visit. This would be the first time I saw Chelsea since that fateful night at the hospital.

Lessons of Resilience and Faith

I walked into my aunt and uncle's house and saw my cousin, Chelsea, sitting on the couch. She was slowly beginning to look like herself. She wasn't as swollen or dark as I remembered, but unfortunately, she still had a feeding tube, and her scars from her surgeries were very noticeable… yet she was here. Seeing her sitting there, battling through everything, was like witnessing a miracle unfold.

Over time, the feeding tube was removed, and she slowly regained her personality. The sparkle in her eyes returned, and her laughter filled the room once more. She still has a long road ahead, but with each obstacle she faces, she demonstrates extraordinary resilience. Her journey has been a testament to the power of faith, determination, and the human spirit.

This experience has taught me invaluable lessons about strength and resilience. No matter how dire the circumstances, there is always hope. Chelsea's story reminds me that our trials do not define us; our responses to them do. We have the power to rise above our challenges and create new narratives for ourselves.

As I reflect on Chelsea's journey, I am inspired to face my own trials with renewed faith and determination. Her story is a powerful reminder that it's not over until God says it's over.

So, whose report will you believe: man's or the Creator of all mankind's?

Reflection Questions

1. Have you ever experienced a moment that shifted your life from ordinary to extraordinary?

_____

_____

_____

_____

_____

_____

_____

How did you cope with the sudden change?

_____

_____

_____

_____

_____

_____

_____

_____

2. How do you handle uncertainty and fear in crisis situations?

_____

_____

_____

_____

_____

_____

_____

_____

_____

_____

_____

_____

_____

_____

_____

_____

_____

_____

_____

3. In what ways can the support of family and loved ones impact your ability to face difficult challenges?

_____

_____

_____

_____

_____

_____

_____

_____

_____

_____

_____

_____

_____

_____

_____

_____

_____

_____

_____

4. What lessons in resilience and strength have you learned from your own life experiences?

_____

_____

_____

_____

_____

_____

_____

_____

How can you apply these lessons to support others going through similar challenges?

_____

_____

_____

_____

_____

_____

_____

_____

_____

Chapter 7

Trials Amid Turmoil: Battling Health and the Workplace

I had always heard the saying, "God gives His toughest battles to His strongest soldiers," but then, I didn't think *that* soldier was *me*. The 2021-2022 school year felt as if it had knocked the wind out of me. Between a new administrator who came in like a wrecking ball, a class that tested every ounce of my patience, and another health scare that would bring many to their knees, it felt like I was living through a real-life version of the song "Only the Strong Survive." But to truly understand how this story unfolded, we need to rewind to a few months before the school year began.

The Unexpected Discovery

After a long day of running errands, I had finally settled into my nightly routine. As I was bathing, my hand brushed against something unfamiliar—a small, hard lump that sent a ripple of unease through my entire being. I tried to dismiss it, attributing it to the natural changes many women experience around a certain time of the month, but the doubt lingered. Later, as I lay in bed, I reached for the spot again, and this time, the lump felt undeniable, like a warning sign that refused to be ignored.

I didn't want to spiral into panic by consulting Google or WebMD, so I decided to leave it alone, hoping it would disappear as mysteriously as it had appeared. But as the days passed, the lump remained—steadfast and unyielding. My initial uncertainty began to morph into genuine fear. I knew breast cancer was the most common cancer among women in the United States, and the memory of my older cousin's battle with the disease crept into my mind. With breast cancer in my family history, I couldn't shake the growing concern.

The following morning, I picked up the phone and called my primary care doctor's office. My voice wavered as I explained that I had discovered something that didn't feel right, yet avoiding the details as if speaking them aloud would make them more real. Due to COVID-19 restrictions and the adjusted office hours, I was given the earliest appointment available, which was a few days later. All I could do was wait, caught in a limbo of worry and reluctant hope.

When I arrived for my appointment, a mix of anxiety and determination settled over me. I explained my concern to the doctor, describing the lump I had discovered. She listened intently and then began the examination, her hands methodically moving across my breast. At first, she didn't feel anything, and I briefly allowed myself to hope that maybe I had overreacted. But when I lay down on the examination table, the angle shifted, and her expression changed. This time, she found the lump. Although she tried to remain composed, I could sense the subtle shift in her demeanor. She was careful not to let her concern show too much, but it was clear she understood the potential seriousness of the situation. Her eyes met mine with a blend of reassurance and unspoken caution.

"I don't want to alarm you," she began, her voice gentle yet steady, "but I think it's important that you see a specialist. Instead of referring you to a local doctor, I'd prefer to send you to someone in Charleston. Are you okay with that?" She added, "This specialist comes highly recommended. In fact, a member of my own family has been treated there, and they received exceptional care."

Without hesitation, I agreed. The drive to Charleston was a small price to pay for peace of mind. I already had a network of doctors in the area, so adding one more to the list didn't feel like an inconvenience. She nodded, relief evident on her face. "I'll take care of everything on my end, and someone from the specialist's office will contact you with the details. Just remember," she added, her tone softening, "don't worry until you're sure there's a reason to worry."

As I left the office, her words echoed in my mind. They were meant to be comforting, but the underlying uncertainty hung over me like a cloud, reminding me that this was just the beginning of a journey I hadn't anticipated.

A few days later, my appointment was scheduled, and when the day finally arrived, a wave of nervousness settled in with it. I'd driven to Charleston countless times and seen numerous doctors, but this appointment felt different. There was a lingering uncertainty. On the one hand, it could be a minor issue, just another footnote in my already extensive medical history; on the other hand, it could be something that might change my life completely. The weight of that uncertainty made me realize I didn't want to face this alone, so I asked a close friend to accompany me. They agreed without hesitation, offering the support I knew I would need.

I arrived at the doctor's office, signed in, and began completing the necessary paperwork. Fortunately, my doctor had already provided much of my medical history, so there wasn't too much left for me to fill out. As I sat in the waiting room, I watched several women get called back, each one heightening my anticipation. Eventually, my name was called.

Once in the exam room, the nurse carefully explained what I could expect during the appointment, ensuring I understood each step. A few moments later, the doctor entered with a calm yet focused demeanor, conducted her exam, and did initial imaging. Afterward, she told me that she would need to perform a biopsy of the area to get a clearer understanding of what we were dealing with. This left me with a mix of apprehension and hope. I would return a few weeks later for the biopsy. Until then, all I could do was pray and wait.

Testing My Teaching Limits

As the school year began a few weeks later, I found myself facing another test of a different kind. This year was quickly shaping up to be one for the books. Over the years, I had gained a bit of a reputation for being assigned the "complex learners" or "heavy hitters" (students who required extra attention, patience, and creative approaches to keep them engaged). I embraced the challenge, but sometimes, I couldn't help but wonder if I truly had the skills to reach them all effectively.

This year, however, was different. My roster was more challenging than any I'd had before. Whether it was because I was the youngest teacher on my team, because I never complained to the administration about my assignments, or simply because someone thought I could handle it, I couldn't say for sure. But as I stared at the names on that list, I knew I was in for a ride.

I still remember a coworker pulling me aside, shaking their head, and saying, "There's no way those students should have all been put together in one class." Their words echoed in my mind as the first day approached, filling me with a mix of dread and determination. I've never been the type of teacher to label students as "troublesome" before meeting them. I always tell my students, "Unless I'm related to you or have taught you before, I really don't know you, and you don't know me, so it's a fresh start for all of us."

That philosophy guided me as I prepared to welcome my new class. I knew the roster was stacked with students who had reputations for being challenging. Yet, I was determined to give each one of them a chance to prove themselves—to start the year with a clean slate. As the first day drew closer, the usual excitement was tinged with an undercurrent of anxiety. I steeled myself, knowing that whatever difficulties lay ahead, I was ready to meet them head-on.

Although we were fully back "in person," this school year was anything but ordinary. It was our first attempt at returning to normalcy after a year of virtual learning, and while we had high hopes, it quickly became clear that "normal" was a moving target. During our teacher workdays before summer break, we spent countless hours planning, trying to piece together a cohesive strategy for the year ahead.

There were originally five of us fifth-grade teachers, and although we'd always been departmentalized, splitting the subjects posed a problem. We couldn't figure out how to ensure that each teacher would be responsible for teaching one of the tested subject areas—ELA/Writing and Mathematics—while still covering everything else. Science and Social Studies weren't on the testing radar that year, so they were lower on the priority list but still essential.

The indecision hung in the air like a thick fog, with none of us eager to break the stalemate. My expertise was in math, a subject I'd taught for the five years I was at the school.

I felt comfortable with it, knew the curriculum inside and out, and had developed a strong rapport with my students on that subject. But deep down, I knew that it probably wasn't possible for me to continue teaching only math.

So, me being me, I "took one for the team." I volunteered to be the self-contained teacher, a role that meant I would teach *all* subjects while the other teachers split the responsibilities. Two of them would take on math and science, while the other two handled ELA and Social Studies. As I made my decision, a wave of uncertainty washed over me, but I was determined to do whatever was needed for the benefit of our students. Little did I know that this choice would set the tone for a year filled with unforeseen hurdles and personal growth.

Challenging Times, Challenging Behaviors

The first days of school arrived, and with them came nineteen fresh-faced fifth-graders, each bringing their own unique energy into the classroom. Among them was one student who at once stood out. "MB" was a young girl with a bold personality and a knack for expressing exactly how she felt about everything—including what she would and would not do.

At first, I tried to manage her behavior on my own, hoping to avoid involving administration. I had several heart-to-heart conversations with MB, trying to understand her point of view and help her adjust to the classroom environment. I also attempted to reach out to her parent, but just as many other educators' phone calls to home, mine also went unanswered.

One day, after returning from recess, MB flatly refused to follow my instructions. By that point, I had done everything I felt I could do, and my patience was wearing thin. I had the rest of the class enter the room, gather their things, and take their seats while I asked her to stay in the hallway. Standing in the doorway, I kept one eye on MB and the other on the class. I asked a coworker who was familiar with MB and her behavior to talk to her. She agreed. Just as the afternoon announcements began, I stepped fully into the room to give my students some final instructions. Moments later, MB reentered the classroom, gathered her belongings, and left with the rest of her classmates at dismissal.

That following Monday, after our routine faculty meeting, the principal approached me and asked if I could stop by her office. I agreed, not thinking much of it. When I walked in, I was met not only by the principal but also by an administrator from another school within the district. The air was heavy with seriousness, and I could sense this would not be an ordinary conversation.

The principal explained the purpose of the meeting: they wanted my insight on an incident that happened the previous week involving MB and a teacher. I recounted the events as clearly as I could and was then asked to provide a typed account of what had happened. I nodded, agreeing to their request without hesitation.

A few days later, on a teacher workday, I found myself back in the office for another meeting—this time with both the principal and the assistant principal. As I sat down, I could feel the tension in the room. I recall the principal asking me if I had witnessed the other teacher "putting their hands on" MB. My answer was an emphatic "No!" I was informed that because I did not follow the school policy on handling the situation with MB, and I also involved another teacher, I would be placed on a very detailed and extensive improvement plan, which would be submitted to the district.

The words felt like a physical blow. I had already reached my breaking point with the situation—MB's constant defiance and blatant disrespect, lack of support from administration, and the countless other classroom challenges that had piled up. And just when I thought it couldn't get worse, there was another blow: because of a surge in COVID-19 cases in our area, things were about to change again.

As if the weight of that wasn't enough, I had received a call over the previous weekend from the breast specialist. She said she needed me to come in to discuss the results of a biopsy I had done and insisted on not talking over the phone. The ominous tone of her voice sent chills down my spine. With everything else going on, this news truly terrified me.

I could feel the walls closing in, and all the pressure and fear finally bubbled over. Before I knew it, I banged my fist on the table and yelled, "I want her out of my class!" The outburst startled my administrators, but the principal, keeping her composure, said they could make that happen. At the conclusion of the meeting, she asked how I felt about the meeting. Still reeling from everything, I replied, "I'm fine, but now I have to go find out if I have breast cancer."

I left for my appointment with the weight of the world on my shoulders and tears streaming down my face. It felt like I had a target on my back, with arrows of doubt, fear, and stress constantly being thrown at me from every direction. I prayed silently as I drove, seeking strength and comfort during this storm. **"The LORD is my shepherd; I shall not want"** **(Psalm 23:1 [NKJV])**, I reminded myself, hoping to find peace in the promise that He was guiding me through this dark valley.

When I arrived at the doctor's office, my heart was pounding, and my hands trembled as I checked in. The wait felt like an eternity, every minute stretching into what felt like hours. Finally, I was called back, and I met with the doctor. She sat me down and calmly explained the results. "Non-cancerous," she said, her voice steady and reassuring. "What you have is a fibroadenoma—a solid, painless, benign breast tumor."

Bent but Not Broken

The moment she said "non-cancerous," I felt as if a massive weight had been lifted off my shoulders. Relief washed over me, and I exhaled deeply, just then realizing how long I had been holding my breath. The months of worry, the sleepless nights, and the constant gnawing fear all melted away in an instant. I finally had an answer, and it wasn't the one I had feared most. "Thank you, LORD," I whispered under my breath, grateful for His mercy and grace that had seen me through this trial.

I returned to work the next day, and true to her word, the principal had removed MB from my classroom. It felt like another massive weight had been lifted from my shoulders. But despite that relief, I was still burdened with the responsibility of completing the improvement plan that had been imposed on me. The plan required me to meet with the principal multiple times a week, which eliminated my planning period. I was also instructed to visit "master" teachers at a nearby school, carefully observe their methods, and write detailed reports on each experience. In addition, I had to complete several modules of a required training program and tackle a series of other assignments—all while managing the demands of teaching multiple subject areas to a class that still had many "complex learners."

The pressure was overwhelming. I was being observed far more frequently than anyone else, with every move I made held under intense scrutiny. Even my students were being questioned about me, as though I were under a microscope. I vividly recall an incident one day during a restroom break. While some students waited, I instructed the class to log onto a website I frequently used to practice math facts—something we had done countless times before. But when the principal walked in, she questioned a few students about the site and, shortly after, sent a school-wide email banning its use altogether. It was a minor incident, but it felt like another blow in what had become a series of relentless stumbling blocks.

As if that weren't enough, one of my grade-level colleagues resigned mid-year, which meant the remaining teachers, including myself, had to absorb additional students into our already full homerooms. The workload increased, the stress mounted, and the year quickly spiraled into the most difficult I had ever experienced.

The following year, I had a conversation that confirmed what I had suspected all along. A colleague confided in me that there had been whispers—subtle implications—that I was incapable of doing my job. Hearing that stung me deeply. It was the validation of the unease I had carried throughout that school year, the feeling that I was being deliberately undermined. It was a test of my resilience—pushing me to my limits, challenging my confidence, and making me question everything. But through it all, I held onto the belief that this trial would not define me. **"I can do all things through Christ who strengthens me" (Philippians 4:13 [NKJV])** *now* became more than just a verse—it became my lifeline. Through faith, I found the strength to keep moving forward, even when it felt impossible.

I seriously contemplated resigning mid-year. How could I possibly succeed in my job when my integrity was constantly under scrutiny? That question echoed in my mind over and over, pushing me to the brink. But each time, I had to remind myself, "This too shall pass." It became a quiet mantra that carried me through the long, exhausting days. Thankfully, the school year eventually came to an end.

In my final meeting with the principal, she acknowledged the resilience I had shown and the personal and professional growth I had achieved. Her words, though well-meaning, felt like a small and almost hollow victory after weathering what felt like a relentless storm. As I walked out of her office for the last time, I realized that true strength isn't about being unafraid—it's about finding the courage to keep going, even when fear threatens to overwhelm you. It's about showing up each day with determination, hope, and the resilience to face whatever hurdles lie ahead. That year had tested me in ways I never expected, but it also revealed a deeper well of strength within me—one that I will carry forward into every new chapter of my life.

Reflection Questions

1. When faced with a challenging situation, how do you usually respond?

    _____

    _____

    _____

    _____

    _____

    _____

    _____

    Do you try to manage it on your own, or do you seek help from others?

    _____

    _____

    _____

    _____

    How has this approach worked for you in the past?

    _____

    _____

    _____

    _____

    _____

2. What was the most challenging experience you've had to face?

_____

_____

_____

_____

_____

_____

How did you get through it?

_____

_____

_____

_____

_____

Looking back, what strengths or coping mechanisms helped you the most during that time?

_____

_____

_____

_____

_____

3. How do you balance taking care of yourself while managing external pressures?

_____

_____

_____

_____

_____

_____

_____

_____

Are there ways you can prioritize self-care, even during the most stressful times?

_____

_____

_____

_____

_____

_____

_____

_____

_____

4. Have you ever felt like you were set up to fail?

_____

_____

_____

_____

_____

_____

_____

_____

_____

How did you navigate that feeling, and what did you learn from the experience?

_____

_____

_____

_____

_____

_____

_____

_____

_____

5. How does your faith or belief system influence how you handle life's storms?

_____

_____

_____

_____

_____

_____

_____

_____

In what ways has it provided comfort or strength during difficult times?

_____

_____

_____

_____

_____

_____

_____

_____

_____

6. Reflecting on a time when you felt overwhelmed, what would you now tell your past self?

_____

_____

_____

_____

_____

_____

_____

_____

What advice or encouragement would you offer?

_____

_____

_____

_____

_____

_____

_____

_____

_____

_____

Chapter 8

A Leap of Faith: Embracing Change and New Opportunities

I n numerology, the number 10 is often associated with new beginnings and cycles of life, marking the completion of one phase and the start of another. The 2022-2023 school year—my 10th year in teaching—embodied this symbolism perfectly. This year ushered in a fresh chapter for me, when I was assigned to teach English Language Arts, a subject I had openly acknowledged was *not* my strongest teaching area. It was a new beginning that pushed me to grow in unexpected ways.

The Year Began "The Five-Year Plan"

By Christmas break 2022, a wave of unhappiness washed over me, leaving me feeling stuck—not in a physical sense, but mentally and emotionally. It was as if I had reached a plateau, and no matter how hard I tried to maintain a confident exterior, the struggles I faced with teaching a new subject were taking their toll. The discontent wasn't just about the difficulties in the classroom; it was more deeply rooted. I was unhappy with myself because I couldn't shake the feeling that something vital was missing, that I was meant to be doing more, achieving more.

The question we're all asked at some point: "Where do you see yourself in five to ten years?" haunted me. I had envisioned a different path, one where I felt fulfilled and aligned with my true purpose. But this? This wasn't it. I couldn't quite pinpoint where I was supposed to be or what I was meant to be doing, but deep down, I knew this wasn't the destination I had in mind. As I wrestled with these thoughts, I remembered a quote by Ralph Waldo Emerson: "Do not go where the path may lead, go instead where there is no path and leave a trail." This quote resonated with me because it reminded me that perhaps I wasn't lost—maybe I was just on the brink of creating my own trail. This realization didn't solve everything, but it gave me a glimmer of hope, a reminder that perhaps this period of uncertainty was just the beginning of a new journey, one where I would finally find what I was searching for.

From an early age, it was ingrained in me to believe that when you don't know where else to turn, you turn to God. Those words echoed in my mind as I found myself at a crossroads, unsure of my next steps. So, I did what I was taught: I prayed. I found a quiet place, away from the noise and distractions, and let my heart pour out. I began by thanking God for all the blessings He had already given me: the strength to face each day, the opportunities that had come my way, and the lessons learned through every trial. But then, with a heavy heart, I asked for guidance. I asked God to reveal the path that I was meant to take, show me where I was truly supposed to be, and what I was meant to do. I prayed for clarity and the courage to follow His lead, even if it meant stepping into the unknown. As I finished my prayer, I felt a small sense of peace—a quiet assurance that, although I didn't have all the answers yet, I was placing my trust in The One who did.

That January, I found myself reflecting on a weekend trip I had taken to Atlanta the previous fall to celebrate a friend's birthday. I had been to Atlanta many times before, but there was something about that trip that felt different, like a subtle shift in the atmosphere I couldn't quite explain. As I recounted the trip, I realized just how deeply that visit had stirred something within me. Atlanta had always been on my radar, but this time, it felt more like a destination and less like a pit stop.

Curiosity began to bubble up inside me, and I started researching everything I could about the city. I already had a network there—my older brother, several line sisters, and other relatives and friends had made Atlanta their home. I reached out to them, asking about their experiences, their neighborhoods, and the rhythms of life in the city. The more I learned, the more I felt drawn to the idea of making Atlanta my new home.

I even took to social media, posing a seemingly casual question "for a friend" about the best school districts in the Metro Atlanta area. But deep down, I knew I wasn't just asking for someone else—I was beginning to map out a potential future for myself. Despite my growing dissatisfaction with teaching, I figured that securing a job in an Atlanta school might be the most straightforward way to make the move. The idea of starting fresh in a new city was both daunting and exhilarating, but I felt a growing conviction that this could be the change I was searching for.

Courage to Consider Possibilities

In March, I heard about a school district in Atlanta that was hosting a job fair later that month. Without hesitation, I packed my bags and set out for Atlanta, filled with nervous energy and a glimmer of hope. The job fair was bustling with activity, a sea of eager candidates and school representatives all vying for the perfect match. I made it a point to network with as many schools as possible, handing out my resume like it was a golden ticket. Each conversation left me feeling more hopeful and more optimistic that this was the beginning of something new. I was told I should expect to hear something within the next few weeks, and that optimism lingered with me long after I left.

Little did I know this would not be my last trip to Atlanta that spring. My older brother was getting married in a few months, and wedding preparations had me traveling back and forth to the city almost every other week. As I reflect on that time, it's clear that Atlanta was becoming more than just a potential move; it was starting to feel like home. I was there so often; it felt like a dress rehearsal for the life I was slowly but surely building.

Over spring break, my phone started buzzing with interview requests. Two schools I had connected with wanted to interview me, and I was thrilled. I packed up again and headed to Atlanta, ready to give it my all. As soon as I arrived, the opportunities multiplied—two more schools contacted me for interviews while I was there! I eagerly agreed. That week was a whirlwind of meetings and conversations, each one adding another layer to the possibility of a new beginning.

By the end of the week, I had completed four interviews, and one school stood out. They offered me a job on the spot! The school was located in an area I knew well, the interview team was warm and welcoming, and the position was for a grade level for which I had experience. It all felt right. But, as with most things, there were formalities to follow. The principal, who had made it clear she wanted me on her team, told me that while she didn't foresee any issues, she still needed to submit the necessary paperwork to the district. She assured me I would hear from them by Monday.

True to her word, the district reached out that Monday, and by the end of the week, I had an official contract. It should have been a moment of pure joy, but instead, I felt a strange sense of uncertainty. As the saying goes, "Sometimes, the things you're most afraid of are the things that will set you free." *This offer was everything I had worked for, so why did I still feel a knot in my stomach?* I knew I should be excited, but a sense of uncertainty lingered in the back of my mind. What should have felt like a moment of victory was instead overshadowed by a flood of doubts. *Was this opportunity truly meant for me, or was it just my desire for change clouding my judgment?* The questions swirled relentlessly. *Was I being guided by purpose, or was I simply trying to escape the familiar, the comfortable?*

Growth and Impact

The weight of the decision bore down on me, as this wasn't the only path available. Beyond the job offer in Atlanta, other doors were open. I could seize this chance and start anew in a city that held so much promise but also so much unknown. Or I could stay where I was, settling for the comfort of routine, even though it no longer fulfilled me. Another option was to remain in my district but take on a different opportunity, perhaps moving to teach at the middle or high school level. And then, there was the possibility of stepping into a new role in a neighboring district, allowing me to stay close to home but still pursue something different.

As I wrestled with these choices, a quote by C.S. Lewis came to mind: "You can't go back and change the beginning, but you can start where you are and change the ending." This decision wasn't just about where I would teach—it was about shaping the next chapter of my life. Each option carried its own risks and rewards, and the choice was ultimately about more than just my career. It was about deciding who I wanted to be and whether I had the strength to change the course of my journey.

I recall a pivotal conversation with a close friend when she asked me a question that seemed simple on the surface but carried profound weight: "Which opportunity do you think will lead to the most growth and have the strongest impact on your life?" The question lingered in the air, demanding an answer that wasn't easy to give. I knew which choice seemed obvious, but fear gripped me. The thought of stepping into something new and unknown felt daunting, even though I was deeply unhappy with my current situation.

Embracing Uncharted Territory

Reflecting on her words now, I'm reminded of something my pastor, Dr. Dharius Daniels, once said about discerning opportunities: "When the enemy cannot destroy us with dysfunction, his next step is to destroy us with distraction. And that distraction can look like an amazing opportunity, but everything that glitters isn't gold." My life at that moment was riddled with dysfunction, and I was desperate for change. Yet, the prospect of something new felt uncomfortable—an uncharted territory that scared me.

I also recalled a close friend's podcast, *Serving It Raw with a Side of Tea*. During the episode "Reclaiming Resilience: Navigating Past Trauma with Grace," I heard the phrase, "Uncomfortable don't feel good." That simple yet powerful statement resonated with me deeply. My current discomfort was pushing me toward change, but I knew that stepping into the unfamiliar would come with its own stressors. Still, I realized that growth often requires us to embrace the discomfort, step into the unknown, and trust that the journey will lead us to where we're meant to be.

As the school year drew to a close, I found myself in a whirlwind of emotions. So once again, I turned to prayer, asking God to quiet my restless thoughts and guide my steps. It's easy to get caught up in our own emotions and make decisions based on our immediate feelings, but I knew I needed to wait for His direction. I asked God to show me the path that was truly meant for me, to reveal the best choice for my life. It wasn't until the very last working day of the school year that I found the clarity I had been praying for. With a mixture of nervous anticipation and newfound faith, I signed the contract to teach in Georgia. I had to step out in faith, trusting that *this* was where He wanted me to be, even if the road ahead seemed uncertain.

Soon after, I found an apartment in Atlanta, packed up my belongings, and prepared to begin my new chapter. The move was more than just a physical relocation; it was a leap of faith, a testament to resilience, and a step toward the life God had prepared for me. I knew this journey wouldn't be easy, but I was ready to embrace the unknown, trusting that each step was part of His greater plan.

Reflection Questions

1. What recent experiences have made you feel stuck or dissatisfied?

_____

_____

_____

_____

_____

_____

_____

_____

How have you responded to those feelings?

_____

_____

_____

_____

_____

_____

_____

_____

2. Have you ever felt drawn to a new beginning, even when it seemed daunting?

_____

_____

_____

_____

_____

_____

_____

_____

What steps did you take to move forward?

_____

_____

_____

_____

_____

_____

_____

_____

3. In what ways do you seek clarity and guidance when faced
   with difficult decisions?

   _____

   _____

   _____

   _____

   _____

   _____

   _____

   _____

   _____

   _____

   _____

   _____

   _____

   _____

   _____

   _____

   _____

   _____

   _____

   _____

4. How do you discern between opportunities that are meant to help you grow and those that may be distractions?

_____

_____

_____

_____

_____

_____

_____

_____

_____

_____

_____

_____

_____

_____

_____

_____

_____

_____

_____

_____

5. Reflect on a time when you had to trust in something greater than yourself to guide you through a challenging situation. What was the outcome?

_____

_____

_____

_____

_____

_____

_____

_____

_____

_____

_____

_____

_____

_____

_____

_____

_____

_____

Chapter 9

Facing the Storm: Resilience and Resolve in the Classroom

New Beginnings

The start of the 2023-2024 school year marked my eleventh year of teaching, a milestone that, in numerology, symbolizes balance. Despite a decade of experience, this year promised to be unlike any before. I found myself in a familiar grade level but a new school, district, and state. As I pulled into the parking lot, the building loomed large, a reminder of the unknown difficulties ahead. I whispered a prayer, asking God to guide me and shape the year according to His will. I stepped into the elevator and ascended to the third floor, each ding echoing my anticipation. After entering my classroom, I began to unpack, fully aware that I was stepping into the unexpected but ready to face whatever lay ahead.

Routine Interrupted

Wednesday, January 31, 2024, began like any other day in my classroom. I adhered to my usual routine as best as I could until it was time to switch classes. My afternoon group was typically more energetic than my morning class, but I was ready for the task. After exchanging classes with my team teacher, I began my ELA lesson as usual. Just a few moments into the lesson, "JC" walked in and took a seat.

As a teacher, I understand that students can be late for a myriad of reasons—finishing an assignment with another teacher, getting called to the front office, or simply attempting to skip class. JC, in particular, had a history of occasional tardiness. When he slipped into the classroom that afternoon, I didn't dwell on it or ask questions. The soft hum of focused students filled the room, and I was engrossed in guiding a small group. JC quietly joined in, blending seamlessly with the others as he got to work. The familiarity of his presence and the routine of the classroom kept the moment unremarkable, just another thread in the fabric of the school day.

Some time passed, and I caught the faint sound of commotion over the walkie-talkie. Although the volume was low, the murmur of conversation was unmistakable. In an elementary school, it could be anything. As the time for lunch approached, I wrapped up my small group session and guided my students through our lunch routine. They put away their materials, placed computers on the cart, gathered their lunchboxes/recess materials, and then sat at their desks, waiting patiently for me to call groups, sections, or numbers to line up. Just as I called the first group, an announcement came over the intercom: we were to go on a soft lockdown.

Soft lockdowns differed from hard lockdowns in that, while we had to lock our doors, we didn't need to hide and could continue with instruction as usual. We were instructed to place color cards beside our doors to indicate whether we had all our students or if any were missing. Unlike emergency lockdowns, where any student caught in the hallway is brought into the nearest room for safety, during this specific lockdown, only those on our rosters were allowed in.

I had my students sit back down and quickly scanned the room to ensure everyone was present. Once I confirmed all my students were accounted for, I placed the corresponding color card outside, closed my door, and locked it. Shortly thereafter, a member of the administration team entered my room to check the color card, verify that no students were missing, and then quietly exited. The air was tense with an undercurrent of unease, yet the routine tasks kept the classroom in a semblance of normalcy.

A female student raised her hand and asked if this was a drill. Given our monthly safety drills, especially in light of recent events involving schools, her concern was understandable. I told her I wasn't sure; however, this wasn't on the school calendar, nor had I received any email notification. Time dragged on, and the lockdown extended well into the students' usual lunchtime and recess.

To keep myself from appearing worried (even though I was truly terrified), I busied myself with grading papers and had the students complete their missing assignments for the week. The classroom buzzed with the soft rustling of papers and the occasional whisper. Another member of the administration team knocked softly on the door, peering in to ask if all my students were present. I confirmed they were and continued my tasks, trying to maintain an air of calm.

Anyone who has worked with children, particularly in an elementary school, knows that keeping them still and focused during uncertain times is a struggle. Every few minutes, a hand would shoot up with a request to go to the restroom or get a drink of water. I knew their curiosity was piqued, and they wanted to understand what was happening, but I had to firmly explain that, for safety reasons, no one could leave the room. The tension in the room was palpable, like a coiled spring, but we carried on, trying to maintain a semblance of normalcy amid the uncertainty.

An Unsettling Presence

Sometime later, a third admin team member entered my room, and this time, her demeanor was different. She glanced directly at where JC was sitting and asked if he had been there the entire time. I explained that he came in late but had been present since before the lockdown began. She nodded and left the room, speaking into her walkie-talkie just outside the door. Moments later, several more admin team members arrived. I overheard JC telling another student, "It's because of me." Without any context of their conversation, I didn't think much of it.

As the minutes ticked by, several students began squirming in their seats, each insisting they needed to use the restroom. Knowing young children well, I could tell their discomfort was genuine. I approached the door and asked if they could be allowed to go. The admin outside agreed, but only in small groups of three or four. I organized the trips, and soon, they returned, visibly relieved.

Then, the atmosphere shifted dramatically. The same admin team member returned, but this time accompanied by three uniformed police officers. Up until that moment, I had managed to keep my composure, but the sight of the officers heightened my anxiety. I could feel my heart pounding, yet I tried to mask my fear to avoid alarming the students. Despite my efforts, their faces betrayed their own fears—especially the girls, some of whom looked on the verge of tears.

One officer walked over to JC, who now had his head down on his desk, and gently asked him to come with them. JC refused, his voice firm. The officer then attempted to help JC up, but the boy became irate and began screaming and resisting. This wasn't the first time JC had a "meltdown." A few weeks earlier, the principal had to physically restrain him from leaving the building during a similar outburst. He had also disrupted my class before by running around and screaming. The familiar chaos of JC's behavior, mixed with the tense presence of the officers, created a surreal and unsettling scene in the classroom.

The officer conferred with his colleagues, and I overheard him mention that they might have to remove JC forcibly. Through the tension, I maintained a composed demeanor, even as many of my students were clearly terrified and some had begun to cry. One of the officers approached me and asked if I would evacuate the students from the classroom.

With as much calm as I could muster, I walked over to the group of girls who were crying. I reassured them that everything would be okay and asked them to quietly go across the hall to my team teacher's classroom. They quickly left— their eyes wide with fear. I then moved to the other groups, repeating the same instructions. Once the last group of students had exited, I was directed to join them and to make sure I closed the door behind me.

Inside the other teacher's classroom, the students sat in stunned silence. I tried to distract them from the chaos outside, but their curiosity and fear were palpable. A few moments later, an admin team member appeared at the door and asked me to bring my students back to our classroom. By now, we had missed our entire lunchtime, and some students began to complain of hunger. We were informed that lunch would be delivered to our classrooms and that the students needed to choose their meal options. Lunch finally arrived, and I did my best to divert the students' attention from the morning's events, although I was still grappling with my own emotions.

We made it through the rest of the school day. With each passing hour, my students seemed to share my increasing sense of restored calm. The distractions of routine classroom activities and assignments ushered us through the afternoon without further discussion about JC. Unfortunately, I was never informed about what happened afterward. *Had he committed a crime? What was the result of the police being involved?* All I could do was say a prayer, thankful for the end of an incident that could have easily escalated into something worse.

After that tumultuous Wednesday, I was eagerly awaiting the end of the week. I had envisioned Friday, February 2nd, as a day of respite. For many, Friday represents a chance to unwind after a hectic week, and I had planned for this day to be a *breather* for both my students and me. With no major assessments scheduled and my policy of avoiding new content on Fridays—since students are often preoccupied with upcoming sports events, celebrations, and the weekend—I was looking forward to a low-key day. If I introduced new material on a Friday, I'd simply need to revisit it on Monday, so why give myself extra work to do? I was confident that this Friday would be the relaxing break we all needed.

Chaos Erupts

The morning began smoothly. I reviewed the day's content, conducted interventions, and switched classes as planned. By 12:25 p.m., it was time for lunch. My students followed their usual routine, and I guided them down to the cafeteria. Teachers were relieved of the duty of supervising lunch, a welcome break that many used for making copies, relaxing in their classrooms, or stepping out to grab lunch. At 12:55 p.m., it was time for recess. While lunch was duty-free, recess was not. We lined up our classes and walked them to the playground. Most students were spread out, some playing soccer, while teachers stationed themselves strategically around the playground to cover all corners in case of an emergency.

Recess was proceeding as usual until a sudden shift disrupted the calm. I noticed a cluster of students darting toward a specific spot on the playground. When I turned to see what was causing the commotion, I saw smoke rising in that direction. As I hurried toward it, I realized a car parked in front of the building was engulfed in flames, billowing thick, gray smoke. I shouted for the students to move back as far as possible.

147

The fire alarms inside the school began blaring, signaling everyone to evacuate. Unlike a standard fire drill, where each grade level has a designated spot, we were simply instructed to move to a safe location. We lined up the students and stood in stunned silence as the situation unfolded.

The flames grew fiercer, and the smoke darkened to an ominous black. I knew it was possible for the car to explode. Sirens wailed in the distance, and then a loud *POP* echoed through the air. The sight of the flames and the sound of the sirens intensified the students' fear. Many were crying, particularly those worried about younger siblings who were also students. I approached a group gathered around a girl who was distressed about her little brother's safety. Her repeated cries of "I don't see my brother or his class" pierced through the chaos. I reassured her with calm words, explaining that her brother's class was on the other side of the building. Even amid such unforeseen circumstances, the resilience and concern of children offer profound lessons in empathy and courage.

A few moments later, the fire trucks arrived, followed closely by an ambulance. The fire was proving difficult for the firefighters to control, with flames stubbornly clinging to the vehicle. Amidst the chaos, I noticed a child being treated by paramedics at the edge of the playground. Later, we learned that this student had suffered an asthma attack triggered by the heightened emotions and the smoke-filled air. The cries of younger students in fear echoed around me, a haunting reminder of their vulnerability.

Soon after, a message was sent through the school's notification app, informing parents that dismissal would be delayed due to the situation. They were reassured that all students were safe and advised not to come to the school for early pickup.

Eventually, the fire was extinguished, though wisps of smoke continued to rise from the charred vehicle. We were informed that it was safe to reenter the building, but only through the rear entrances. The younger students were led inside first, followed by the older ones. Since we had been on the playground for recess, I instructed my students to gather their belongings before we left. Back in the classroom, a heavy silence settled over the room as students sat in quiet fear and concern.

The principal's voice crackled over the intercom, praising everyone for ensuring the safety of the students and announcing that dismissal would proceed as usual, with exceptions for those in specific after-school programs. As the bells signaled the end of the day, we supervised the students' exit. Through the windows, everyone's attention was drawn to the smoldering car parked outside. The scent of smoke lingered in the air as students headed to their buses or carpool locations.

Shortly after the buses left and carpools ended, we were instructed to gather in the gym for an impromptu meeting. All faculty and staff members assembled, their faces a mix of concern and exhaustion. The principal stood at the front and provided a detailed explanation of the incident, her voice steady as she addressed the gravity of the situation. She fielded numerous questions, responding as thoroughly as possible to reassure us.

As the meeting concluded and the staff began to disperse, one of my coworkers approached me with a look of empathy. "Breland, if you need to take a day off on Monday, I understand. This week has been a lot for you," she said, her tone gentle and understanding.

I managed a weary smile and replied, "I know, right?" The enormity of the week's events began to weigh heavily on me as I left the gym.

Exiting the building, I felt the week's tension pressing down on me. I entered my car and sat behind the wheel, the silence of the enclosed space offering a brief respite. The moment the door closed, my emotions surged, and I finally allowed myself to feel the full impact of the stress, fear, and exhaustion that had accumulated throughout the week.

Field Trip

Thursday, March 14th, was an exciting day for the fifth-graders. It was field trip day, and if you can remember school field trips, you'd recall the thrill of no schoolwork, leaving the school building, and taking a break from the everyday routine. For elementary students, field trips are a burst of joy, a chance to explore new places and experiences. As a teacher, while it's rewarding to expose students to new environments, the anticipation of a field trip can be nerve-wracking.

Don't get me wrong. We love the break from our normal routine and the opportunity to see our students' eyes light up with excitement. But behind the scenes, there's a whirlwind of planning and anxiety. Ensuring that all students who aren't attending have proper assignments, being prepared for any emergency medical needs, and constantly making sure that every child is accounted for adds layers of stress to the day.

That morning, the air buzzed with excitement. The students arrived earlier than usual, chattering about the day ahead. They wore their brightest smiles, and their eyes sparkled with anticipation. As we lined up to meet with the principal in the cafeteria, the usual chatter turned into an excited roar. Each child clutched their permission slips and packed lunches like treasures.

After the principal's comments to the students and the distribution of name badges, we were officially ready. We, the teachers, did our final headcount, double-checking lists and emergency contact information. There was a palpable mix of excitement and tension among us. With everything in place, we exited the building, each teacher and accompanying chaperone taking a deep breath, ready to embrace the day's chaos and joy.

Since the field trip destination was close to the school, it was decided beforehand that we would walk instead of taking buses. Thankfully, the weather was perfect for our journey. The sky was clear; the sun was shining, and there was a gentle breeze, making it an ideal day for a stroll. The local police department accompanied us, blocking intersections and occasionally playing a friendly game of rock-paper-scissors with the students as we crossed. After a 25-minute walk filled with laughter and excitement, we finally arrived at the theater.

In ELA, we had been studying dramas, so a trip to the theater to watch a live performance was a perfect complement to our lessons. We had discussed the features of a drama in class, so it was thrilling to hear my students recognize and talk about them as we watched the production. The theater was alive with vibrant sets and energetic actors, and the students were captivated. The highlight of the performance was a young child actor who stole the show. At the conclusion, our students joined the audience in a standing ovation, their cheers echoing through the theater.

After the performance, we waited for the students to use the restroom and then conducted final headcounts. It was time to head back to school, and we followed the same routine as we did that morning. The police escorted us, ensuring our safe passage. Because we returned earlier than expected, we were able to have lunch in the cafeteria. The students were still buzzing with excitement from the field trip, and our usual schedule was completely off, so we decided to extend recess.

The students quickly finished their lunches, eager to get outside. The playground was a scene of joy and energy as they ran, played, and shared their favorite moments from the theater. It was a perfect end to an exciting day, a reminder of the joy and learning that can come from stepping outside the classroom and into the world.

It was time to head back inside. We lined the students up by class as usual and began our walk to the building. A few students had already entered when I saw fear in their faces and heard them frantically calling my name. I quickly walked over, trying to calm them down, as they told me that a student in my class had a knife. I asked which student, and they pointed him out. It was hard to believe—this particular student was never a troublemaker and was always helpful in class.

I approached him and asked if he had something that shouldn't be at school. He looked confused and said, "No." Not seeing anything in his hands and knowing book bags were in the classroom, I asked if he had something in his pocket. He hesitated and then said, "Yes." I asked him to show it to me. He pulled out a metallic object and pressed a button, revealing a long, sharp blade. My heart pounded, and every thought possible filled my mind. At that moment, my team teacher was walking into the building. I asked him to take the students to class while I handled a situation.

This was beyond anything I had ever dealt with, and I knew I had to report it immediately. I asked the student if the knife was his, if he had found it, or if someone had given it to him. With each question, he simply shrugged his shoulders. Frustrated and needing answers, I took the knife and headed to the assistant principal's office. She was busy with another situation, so she directed me to the principal.

When I arrived at the office with the student, the principal met me at the door. She knew I was coming and asked what was happening. I showed her the knife. She looked at it gravely and said it was serious, potentially leading to expulsion. She asked the student some questions, but he remained unresponsive. I explained the situation to her, and she assured me they would handle it.

Returning to my classroom, I thanked my team teacher for covering and informed him that I hadn't gotten any answers from the student. Realizing he was missing, a few of my students asked about their classmate. I reassured them that he was alright, and everything was okay. The final bell rang, and I followed our normal dismissal routine, escorting the students to their respective locations. After the buses left, I returned to my empty classroom.

As I sat at my desk with my head down, the weight of the day's events pressed down on me while fear, anger, and frustration welled up inside me. The day had started with such excitement and joy, but it ended with an unsettling and serious incident. It was a stark reminder of the unpredictability of our roles as educators, where joy and crisis can, unfortunately, coexist within the same day.

Now, as I reflect on the year, I realize that each event, no matter how daunting, had a silver lining. The chaos of the soft lockdown and JC's outburst revealed the importance of staying composed under pressure. The harrowing sight of the burning car during recess reminded me of the vital role we, as educators, play in ensuring the safety and well-being of our students. The eye-opening incident with the knife highlighted the profound responsibility we have in guiding and protecting the young lives entrusted to us.

Resilience, I learned, isn't about remaining unscathed by life's challenges but about bending without breaking. It's about finding strength in vulnerability and clarity in chaos. It's about recognizing that while we may be shaken, we can still stand tall and carry on. In the end, it's not about the absence of storms but about learning to dance in the rain, to bend but not break, and to arise stronger from each trial.

Reflection Questions

1. **Facing the Unexpected:**

   Think about a time when you were faced with an unexpected challenge.

   How did you initially react?

   _____

   _____

   _____

   _____

   _____

   _____

   What steps did you take to manage the situation?

   _____

   _____

   _____

   _____

   _____

   _____

   _____

2. **Building Resilience:**

In what ways can you cultivate resilience in your own life?

_____

_____

_____

_____

_____

_____

Identify both minor daily practices and major strategies for overcoming significant obstacles.

_____

_____

_____

_____

_____

_____

_____

_____

_____

_____

_____

3. **Support Systems:**

Who are the people or resources that form your support system?

_____

_____

_____

_____

_____

_____

How can you strengthen these connections to better prepare for future challenges?

_____

_____

_____

_____

_____

_____

_____

_____

_____

4. **Staying Calm Under Pressure:**

Reflect on and note a situation when you had to remain calm despite feeling anxious or scared.

_____

_____

_____

_____

_____

_____

_____

_____

What techniques did you use to maintain your composure?

_____

_____

_____

_____

_____

_____

_____

_____

5. **Learning from Adversity:**

Identify a difficult experience that ultimately taught you a valuable lesson.

_____

_____

_____

_____

_____

_____

_____

_____

How has this lesson influenced your approach to new challenges?

_____

_____

_____

_____

_____

_____

_____

_____

6. **Creating a Safe Environment:**

As seen in this chapter, maintaining a calm and safe environment was crucial.

How can you create a supportive and secure atmosphere in your own community or workplace?

_____

_____

_____

_____

_____

_____

_____

_____

_____

_____

_____

_____

_____

_____

_____

_____

7. **Faith and Resilience:**

How does your personal faith or belief system contribute to your resilience?

_____

_____

_____

_____

_____

_____

_____

In what ways can you draw on these beliefs during times of difficulty?

_____

_____

_____

_____

_____

_____

While reflecting on these questions, uncover your own strengths and strategies for resilience and better prepare yourself for life's inevitable storms.

Chapter 10

A New Beginning: Trusting the Journey Ahead

A s the final days of the academic year approached, I found myself feeling both liberated and terrified. I was grappling with a whirlwind of emotions. For years, teaching had been my anchor, my sense of purpose, and my security. Now, I was standing at a crossroads, unsure of where life would take me next.

Silent Struggles

Teaching had always been my dream. I loved children, cherished learning, and found true joy in helping others discover new knowledge. But in recent years, that joy and peace began to slip away. The profession became increasingly entangled in politics and standardized testing, slowly choking the passion that had once fueled me. After COVID-19, the pressures mounted—fighting not just for my students but also against the weight of expectations from parents and administrators and the relentless demands of a system that was undeniably broken. The panic attacks, stress, and other medical concerns only added to the burden. For years, I wrestled with the growing realization that teaching, as it had become, no longer fulfilled me. Yet, I maintained the façade, forcing a smile even when it felt like the hardest thing to do. In teacher preparation classes and professional development sessions, we were always told to "show up" for the students, to be happy for them, and to smile for them. And I did— faithfully. *But what happens when you no longer have the strength to do that?*

One morning, as I pulled up to the school building, I turned off the car and simply cried. The weight of my weariness finally broke through. I wiped my tears, gathered my things, and forced myself to enter the building. Once inside my classroom, the tears came again. But as the students began to file in, I wiped my face, put on that well-practiced smile, and welcomed them.

Children, with their innocent perception, see more than we often realize. Even though I tried to hide my struggle, some of them sensed it. As they were about to leave for their related arts classes, one student quietly dropped a note on my desk. After walking them to their destination, I returned to my empty classroom and unfolded the note. Among the words

166

written, one line struck me deeply: "Your belief in me makes me believe in myself." In that moment, I realized that despite the exhaustion and doubts, my presence still mattered to them. It was a bittersweet reminder of why I had become a teacher in the first place and how difficult it was to let go of something that had been such a fundamental part of me.

Teaching is a calling, a true passion, and I am forever grateful for every student who walked through my door. *But how could I continue when I no longer felt the fire within?* The verse from **Ecclesiastes 3:1 (NKJV) resonates with me: "To everything, *there* is a season, and a time to every purpose under heaven."** My season of teaching was coming to an end, and it was time to embrace a new chapter, one where I could rediscover my passion and purpose.

My Last Day

May 24, 2024, marked my official last day. I still remember the moment I walked out of the school building for the final time. My classroom, once bustling with the energy of students and the hum of learning, now stood eerily silent and spotless, just as I had found it in July. Desks and chairs were neatly stacked along the walls, bulletin boards were stripped bare, and all traces of my presence had been meticulously erased. I had already made several trips to my car, each time laden with totes filled with personal items that had accumulated over the school year—mementos, books, and the small comforts that made the space my own. Now, all that remained was a rolling cart carrying the last few items from my desk.

With a deep breath, I grabbed the handle of the cart, turned off the lights, and walked out of the classroom, the door clicking shut behind me with a finality that echoed through the empty halls. I bid my team farewell, their faces reflecting a mix of emotions, and made my way toward the elevator. I stepped inside, and as I rode down to the main lobby, I couldn't help but feel a strange mix of relief and sadness.

Reaching the second floor, I handed in my keys and submitted my checkout sheet, the final tasks that would officially close this chapter of my life. Once again, I entered the elevator, but this time with a sense of finality that weighed heavier than before. When the doors opened on the first floor, I stepped out, walked through the lobby, and pushed open the front doors of the building, letting the warm air of late spring wash over me.

As I packed the last of my belongings into the car, the reality of it all began to sink in. It felt surreal, knowing I would never again report to this building for work and never again walk these halls. I backed out of the parking space, taking one last glance at the building in my rearview mirror before driving away—the school slowly disappearing from sight as I moved forward into the next chapter of my life.

But what was next? Only God knew.

I'm Done. Now What?

In my classroom, for those students who finished early, I had a board labeled "I'm done, now what?" It was my solution to the constant chorus of "I'm done. Now, what do I do?" It was a way to guide them to the next task without missing a beat. But now, as I stand at my own crossroads, I find myself asking the same question: "God, I'm done. Now what?" It's funny how life brings you full circle, leaving you staring at the very board you created, seeking direction for the next step in your own journey.

I vividly remember one Sunday morning, sitting in the lobby of my church, when a profound realization struck me like a ton of bricks. As I sat there, the words seemed to resonate in my mind: "Everyone has a story to tell." It was as if a door had opened within me, and suddenly, thoughts and ideas began to flood in, swirling around in my mind, demanding to be put into words. The clarity of that moment was undeniable—I *knew* I had to share my own story. I reached out to someone who knew someone, and before I knew it, I was putting pen to paper, pouring my heart into this book… one chapter at a time.

As I began to write, the stories flowed more easily than I expected, each sentence peeling back layers of my own experiences and emotions. With every story recounted, and each lesson learned, I found myself revisiting moments of joy, pain, and growth—moments that had shaped me into who I was. Writing became a form of therapy, a way to process all I had been through and find meaning in the struggles I had faced. It wasn't just about telling my story; it was about finding healing and offering hope to others who might be facing their own storms. The more I wrote, the more I realized this book was not just a project—it was a *calling*, a new chapter in my life that was unfolding with each word I put on the page.

Writing this book has stirred up a whirlwind of emotions—stress, doubt, confusion, and endless questioning. I've often found myself wondering if this was truly the path I was meant to take or if I should retreat to the familiarity of the classroom. There's a strange comfort in the chaos of preparing for a new school year, even with its unpaid hours and countless trips for supplies. But now, without that routine, I'm left questioning whether I'm straying from God's plan or following it more closely than ever. A part of me clings to Dr. Martin Luther King, Jr.'s words: "Faith is taking the first step even when you don't see the whole staircase." Here I am, stepping out on faith, trusting that, in time, everything will make sense.

In this season of discovery, I'm choosing to press through by embracing the unknown and trusting the process. It's not easy, but I've learned that resilience isn't about having all the answers—it's about moving forward despite the lack of clarity. It would be so easy to retreat into the familiar chaos of comfort and complacency. Understand, I'm not saying I haven't considered returning to the classroom until I find my "next" because I have, but I'm choosing to keep exploring, to keep searching for what comes next.

During this transition, I'm focusing on staying grounded. This break has granted me an unexpected freedom—freedom to have slow mornings, to choose my own path each day instead of following a strict routine, and to explore new opportunities. My days are anchored by routines that bring me peace, like morning devotionals and journaling. I lean on affirmations that remind me of my strength and purpose, and I draw solace from scriptures that speak directly to my heart.

I'm deeply grateful for my friends who walk alongside me in this season, holding me accountable and reminding me of the journey I'm on. They have become a vital part of my foundation, helping me stay grounded when doubt tries to creep in. Above all, my faith in God keeps me steady, knowing that He is guiding my steps. As **Psalm 119:105 (NKJV) says, "Your word *is* a lamp to my feet And a light to my path."** Even when the way ahead is dim, I trust that each step will be illuminated at the right time, and I move forward with confidence, knowing that God's timing is always perfect.

Reflecting on this current season of my life and all the obstacles I've faced before, I'm reminded of a story I once heard, although the details are hazy. It was about a family caught in a violent thunderstorm during a road trip—lightning flashing, thunder roaring, and rain so heavy that visibility was nearly zero. While many drivers pulled over, hazard lights flashing, the father kept driving, determined to move forward despite the urging of those around him to stop and wait it out.

He kept pressing on, and eventually, the storm was behind them.

That story has stayed with me over the years, becoming a guiding metaphor for my own journey. Life's storms can be relentless, obscuring the path ahead and tempting us to stop in our tracks. But I've learned that by pressing on, no matter how overwhelming the storm may seem, it will eventually pass, leaving clearer skies ahead. Every struggle I have faced has taught me that resilience isn't just about weathering the storm—it's about moving through it, knowing that peace will come once the clouds have cleared.

And so, as I close this chapter of my life, I do so with a heart full of faith and a spirit ready to face whatever lies ahead. The journey is far from over, but I'm committed to pressing on, trusting that the next steps will reveal themselves as they're meant to. Resilience has been my guide, and faith my anchor.

Now, with the raging storm behind me, I'm ready to embrace the calm and the new beginnings it brings.

Reflection Questions

1. How have the storms in your life shaped your understanding of resilience?

---

2. What does "stepping out in faith" look like for you in this season of uncertainty?

_____

_____

_____

_____

_____

_____

_____

_____

_____

_____

_____

_____

_____

_____

_____

_____

_____

_____

_____

_____

3. In what ways can you embrace the unknown while staying grounded in your values and beliefs?

_____

_____

_____

_____

_____

_____

_____

_____

_____

_____

_____

_____

_____

_____

_____

_____

_____

_____

4. How do you find peace in moments of transition?

_____

_____

_____

_____

_____

_____

_____

_____

_____

_____

What practices help you stay anchored?

_____

_____

_____

_____

_____

_____

_____

_____

_____

5. What new beginnings are you ready to embrace?

_____

_____

_____

_____

_____

_____

_____

_____

_____

_____

How will you approach them with the lessons you've learned?

_____

_____

_____

_____

_____

_____

_____

_____

The following are excerpts from the book that specifically address resilience.
I hope they will serve as quick but powerful reminders to you *never* to give up.

❧ ❧ ❧ ❧ ❧

Resilience – What It *Is* and What It *Isn't*

❖ Resilience *is* a special happening, an inner strength that enables us to bend without breaking. It reminds us that no matter how dire the circumstances, the human spirit is capable of extraordinary things.

❖ Resilience *isn't* just about bouncing back; it's about growing through adversity, finding strength in the connections we forge, and embracing the journey with an open heart.

❖ Resilience *isn't* about never facing difficulties; it's about how you confront them and find strength in moments of weakness. Each experience taught me to appreciate the small victories and to hold on to hope, even when the path ahead seemed uncertain.

❖ True resilience *is* born not from the circumstances we encounter but from our ability to adapt, persevere, and find strength within ourselves and each other. With these insights, I was ready to face

179

whatever obstacles the future held, knowing I could overcome anything.

❖ Resilience *is* hope. No matter how dire the circumstances, there is always hope. Chelsea's story reminds me that our trials do not define us; our responses to them do. We have the power to rise above our challenges and create new narratives for ourselves.

❖ Resilience *isn't* about being unafraid. As I walked out of my principal's office for the last time, I realized that true strength isn't about being unafraid—it's about finding the courage to keep going, even when fear threatens to overwhelm you. It's about showing up each day with determination, hope, and the resilience to face whatever challenges lie ahead.

❖ Resilience *isn't* about remaining unscathed by life's challenges but about bending without breaking. It's about finding strength in vulnerability and clarity in chaos. It's about recognizing that while we may be shaken, we can still stand tall and carry on. In the end, it's not about the absence of storms, but about learning to dance in the rain, to bend but not break, and to arise stronger from each trial.

❖ Resilience *isn't* about having all the answers. In this season of discovery, I'm choosing to press through by embracing the unknown and trusting the process. It's not easy, but I've learned that being resilient doesn't mean I'll have all the answers—it's about me moving forward despite the lack of clarity.

Acknowledgments

This book would not have been possible without the incredible support, love, and encouragement of so many amazing people who have touched my life.

First and foremost, I thank God for being my constant source of strength, grace, and guidance. You have walked with me through every challenge, and Your unwavering presence has made this dream a reality. I am forever grateful for Your love and faithfulness.

To my family—your love and belief in me have been the foundation of everything I've accomplished. Mom, your sacrifices, prayers, and endless support have carried me through my toughest days. You are my greatest blessing, and I can't thank you enough for being my rock and my biggest inspiration.

To my best friend and sister-at-heart, Brittany—thank you for always being in my corner. You've been my motivator, my voice of reason, and my biggest cheerleader. Whether I needed tough love or a gentle reminder of my worth, you've been there. I'll always treasure your unwavering support.

To my writing team—thank you for helping me bring this vision to life. Your creativity, dedication, and belief in this project have made all the difference. This book wouldn't be what it is without your incredible talents.

And to everyone who has believed in me, encouraged me, or simply reminded me to keep going—thank you for being part of my story. Your kindness, support, and belief in my potential mean more to me than words can ever express.

With all my love and gratitude,

Megan

About the Author

Megan Sharisse is an author, educator, and advocate for resilience and empowerment. With more than a decade of experience in the classroom, she has dedicated her career to inspiring and supporting learners of all ages. Her passion for education, combined with advanced studies in Elementary Education and Teaching and Learning, has shaped her ability to connect with others and guide them through challenges with grace and determination.

Drawing from her experiences as a teacher and the life lessons she has gained through triumphs and struggles, Megan seeks to inspire others to uncover their inner strength and embrace transformation in the face of adversity.

When she's not writing, Megan enjoys serving in her church, volunteering in the community, and spending time with her family and friends. She is passionate about helping others overcome obstacles, find grace during hardships, and unlock their potential. You can connect with Megan on Instagram at @megansharisse.